# WALKS IN THE
# LLŶN PENINSULA
## Part 2

Walks with History

# Walks in the Llŷn Peninsula

## Part 2
### North and East

## Nigel Burras and Jeff Stiff

*ISBN: 0-86381-365-8*

*Cover: Alan Jones*

*First published in 1996 by Gwasg Carreg Gwalch,
Iard yr Orsaf, Llanrwst, Gwynedd, Wales.
☎ 01492 642031*

*Printed and published in Wales*

# Contents

## Acknowledgements

Grateful thanks are due to Christine Stiff for 'Inputting' on the word processor, and to Marjorie Woodcock for proof reading and suggestions, not forgetting her mother, Mary Rowlands of Edern, for information on Edern mill.

# INTRODUCTION

This is a book of walks, but as it also deals with a wide range of historical and pre-historical times and subjects it is proposed, as in the companion volume, to give a brief introductory account of the main pre-historic and historic periods which may be unfamiliar to some readers.

Most of us, especially when on holiday, enjoy a good country walk, the Llŷn peninsula abounds with them. When out walking and admiring the scenery, many of us would like to know a little of the history of any features, buildings or ancient monuments which they may come across. This book is an attempt to cater for these people, it is written by two local historians who are also avid walkers. The area featured in the following pages, is littered with features of historic interest and covers all periods from the Stone-age to the Modern.

The walks we describe vary in length and terrain to suit both the casual ambler and the dogged countryside tramper. We also bring to the attention of the reader some observations made on the area by travellers in the past, it is enlightening and often amusing to make modern-day comparisons of the area described by eye witnesses some two centuries ago. The quotes used are left unaltered and unadorned.

The retreat of the Glaciers around 12,000 B.C. saw the end of the pre-historic period known as the Paleolithic (*Paleo* — 'old' *lithos* — 'stone') and the emergence of the Mesolithic (*Meso* — 'middle') period which saw the arrival in Llŷn of nomadic hunting tribes. Then followed in around 3000-3500 B.C. the age known as the Neolithic (*neo* — 'new'). This was the first period of permanent settlement and farming in the area. After the Neolithic Stone Age comes the Bronze Age around 1500 B.C. and the first use of metal tools. The Iron Age arrived with the coming of the Celts around 500 B.C. and their war-like tribal society. The Celtic Iron Age with its heroic deeds of war, raid and plunder so wonderfully evoked in some of the early Celtic literature which survived in oral tradition to be written down in the Middle Ages, was brought to a close with the arrival around a half century before the birth of Christ, of the

Romans. Then follows over four centuries of the Romano/British period. The collapse of the Roman Empire and the withdrawal of the legions from Britain in the early years of the 5th century saw the onset of the Dark Ages, the Age of Arthur, a tumultuous period of Saxon invasion and British resistance. This resulted in the final overthrow of the area which is now England by the invaders, leaving Wales and Scotland as the 'Celtic fringe' and stronghold.

When the Romans left Wales they left behind a scene of political turmoil. It is this era that saw the origin of the kingdom of Gwynedd. A certain chieftain named Cunedda came to North Wales from the Strathclyde area of southern Scotland, known as 'Manaw of the Gododdin'. In the early 5th century Cunedda came with his tribe and warband, along with several other leaders traditionally regarded as his sons. This area at the time was largely settled by the Irish but Cunedda soon exercised military dominance over them. The result was the formation of the kingdom of Gwynedd. In accordance with the customs of Welsh inheritance, the newly formed kingdom was divided up amongst his sons. These sub-kingdoms, named after his sons, are thus the earliest of any administrative districts in Gwynedd. Thus, Rhufoniog was the land assigned to Rhufon, or Romanus; Dunoding was the land of Dunawd, or Donatus; Dogfeiling the tribal territory of Dogfael; Ceredigion of Ceredig, Edeyrnion of Edern, or Eternus; Osmael gives his name to Osmaeliaun, a district in Anglesey. Another two sons Cafflog and Einion are commemorated in Llŷn. Cafflogion is the name of a commote comprising the area from Llanengan to Pwllheli, on the southern side of the peninsula (*see fig 2*). Einion is remembered in Llanengan church.

Quite why Cunedda came to this area is not known, the only written source we have, dates from the 9th century and is therefore recording events long in the past. It has been conjectured that he was a strongly romanised chieftain (some of his sons bore romanised names) and that he was sent to North Wales by the Romans in a last gasp effort to leave the country in some sort of order, he may have been instructed to oust the Irish barbarians and establish control in the name of the Roman Empire. He may, alternatively, just have been taking advantage of the power vacuum present in North Wales to establish a new kingdom for himself.

1066 saw the coming of the Normans, and shortly after this, inroads were made by newly established 'Marcher barons' into Wales from areas such as Rhuddlan, Chester, Shrewsbury and Hereford. This period is followed by the Age of the Welsh Princes in the 12th and 13th centuries, with eventual confrontation with Edward I, King of England. Wales finally submitted to defeat — physically at least! — to Edward's forces in 1284.

There will also be from time to time in this book, references to some of the less common plants and animals that are to be found in this very special area. It is an attempt to bring local knowledge to what is already a superb area in which to walk.

Armed, as you will be, with information on where to look and find these treasures of the Llŷn, be sure as you go about your journeys to leave everything as you find it and only your footsteps as evidence of your passing.

It may at this juncture be prudent to say something about the footwear that could be comfortably worn on these walks: It is always wise when in the country to wear boots or at least walking shoes, especially when on the cliff-top paths, of which there are many in this book. It may also be of benefit to remember that although you will probably be walking in the summer, the ground can become very boggy in places. Although if this is likely to be the case you will find that it will have been mentioned, in wet weather the ground in some places can quickly become water-logged, so take care.

If you get as much enjoyment reading and walking with this as we did in writing it, we will have done our job and you will have gained a greater appreciation of an area that has captivated people over many centuries and for many reasons. Happy walking!

# Rights of Way
# A Brief Guide To The Law

### 1. What is a right of way?

A right of way in the countryside can be either a footpath, a bridleway or a byway. On *footpaths* the public has a right of way on foot only. Whereas on *bridleways* the public also have a right of way on horseback and pedal cycles. *Byways* are open to all classes of traffic, including motor vehicles. Legally, a public right of way is part of the Queen's highway and subject to the same protection in law as all other highways, including trunk roads.

### 2. What are my rights on a public right of way?

The public has a right to pass and repass along the way. You can also take with you a 'natural accompaniment', which includes a dog. However, you should ensure that dogs are under close control. On suitable paths, a 'natural accompaniment' could also include a pram or a pushchair.

### 3. How do I know whether a path is a public right of way or not?

The safest evidence is the definitive map of public rights of way. These maps are available for public inspection at county, district and outer London borough council offices. Some are also available for inspection in libraries and some are sold by the councils concerned. In addition, public rights of way information derived from these maps, is shown by the Ordnance Survey on its pathfinder (1:25,000) and Landranger (1:50,000) maps. But note that a path not shown on the definitive map may still be a public right of way, and application may be made to the surveying authorities for ways to be added to the definitive map.

### 4.How does a path become public?

In legal theory, most paths become rights of way because the owner 'dedicates' them to public use. In fact very few paths have been formally dedicated, but the law assumes that if the public uses a path without interference for upwards of 20 years then the owner intends dedication. Most public paths came about this way. But it is not true that a path can cease to be public if it is unused for 20 years (except in Scotland). The legal maxim is 'once a highway, always a highway'. Paths can also be created by agreement between local authorities and owners or by compulsory order, subject, in the case of objection, to the consent of the Secretary of State for the Environment (or for Wales).

## 5. What about crops growing on or over a path?

The farmer has a duty to prevent a crop (other than grass) from making the path difficult to find or follow. You have every right to walk through crops growing on or over a path, but you must stick as close as you can to its correct line. Report the problem to the highway authority: it has the power to prosecute the farmer or cut the crop and send him the bill.

## 6. What is an obstruction on a path?

Anything which interferes with your right to proceed along it, e.g. a barbed wire fence across the path or a heap of manure dumped on it. Dense undergrowth is not normally treated as an obstruction but is dealt with under path maintenance.

## 7. Can I remove an obstruction to get by?

Yes, provided that:
a) you are a bona fide traveller on the path and have not gone out for the specific purpose of moving the obstruction.
b) you remove only as much as is necessary to get through. If you can easily go round the obstruction without causing any damage, then you should do so. But report the obstruction to the highways authority.

## 8. What is a misleading notice?

A misleading notice is one calculated to deter you from using a public right of way, for example, a notice saying 'Private' at the point where a public footpath enters a park. Such notices should be reported immediately to the highway authority. They are illegal on paths shown on the definitive map.

### 9. What is trespass?

The civil tort of trespass arises from the bare fact of unauthorised entry. However, unless injury to the property can be proven, a landowner could probably only recover nominal damages by suing. But of course you might have to meet the landowner's legal costs. Thus a notice saying 'Trespassers will be prosecuted', aimed for instance at keeping you off a private drive, is usually meaningless. Prosecution could only arise if you trespass and damage property. However, under public order law, trespassing with an intention to *reside* may be a criminal offence under some circumstances. It is also sometimes a criminal offence to trespass on military training land.

# Countryside code

The above stated laws represent the footpath users rights, but it should be borne in mind that when these paths cross private or farm land, you have a duty to respect the privacy and/or commercial interests in this land. For this reason we present a few points which constitute a country code which will ensure an harmonious usage between land owner and walker:

1. Please ensure that all field gates are left as you found them.

2. On a footpath through a field, always keep to the edge unless the path is clearly marked across it.

3. Make sure that you do not disturb any livestock in the field, i.e. all dogs should be kept on leads and children kept under control.

4. Take care not to trample any growing crops.

5. Do not remove any large sticks etc, from hedgerows as this could create a gap allowing livestock to escape.

6. Leave any plants and flowers where walkers after you can admire them.

7. Take all your litter away with you.

8. Help to keep all water clean, as any stream may be supplying water to households and/or livestock.

9. Guard against fire risk.

10. Don't make unnecessary noise.

11. Always keep to the designated path.

12. Always use the gates and stiles provided (hopefully!) when crossing fences, hedges or walls.

13. Please ensure when parking your car that it does not obstruct field gates etc.

Please remember when enjoying your countryside walk not to destroy the very thing you came to see.

## CAR ROUTES TO WALK STARTING POINTS

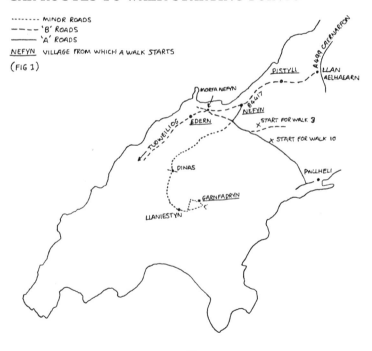

# A Glossary of Welsh Names

Abaty ........................... Abbey
Aber..................... River-mouth
Ardal...........................District
Bach ............................. Small
Bangor............Consecretal land,
                        Monastery
Bedd ............................. Grave
Betws ......... Prayer house, Chapel
Blaenau ....................... Upland
Bod............................. Abode
Bryn................................ Hill
Bwlch............................. Pass
Bychan ......................... Small
Caban ............................ Hut
Cader .............. Seat, Stronghold
Cantref ......... District, Hundred
Caer....................... Fort, Camp
Capel ...........................Chapel
Castell ..........................Castle
Cefn............................. Ridge
Celli..............................Grove
Clas .................. Mother Church
Coch ............................... Red
Craig ............................. Crag
Crib ........................... Summit
Crwth ......................... Fiddle
Cwm ........................... Valley
Cymru ....................... Wales
Cymry..................... The Welsh
Din ............................ Hillfort
Dinas ................ Hillfort, Town
Drwg........................ Bad, Evil
Du................................. Black
Dŵr .............................Water
Dyffryn ......................... Valley
Eglwys........................Church
Esgob ...........................Bishop
Ffin ......................... Boundary
Ffordd ...........................Road
Ffridd..... Sheepwalk, high pasture
Ffynnon ............... Well, Spring

Glan ....................... Riverbank
Glas ...................... Green, Blue
Glyn...................... Glen, Valley
Gwaun.................... Upland bog
Gwely............. Bed, hence family
                        Settlement
Gwlad ....................... Country
Gwyn ..................... White, fair
Hafod............. Summer dwelling
Hen ..................................Old
Hendref.... Old Township, Winter
                        Settlement
Heol, Hewl......................Road
Is ................................Below
Llan....................Church, Place
Llanerch ........................ Glade
Llech ..................... Stone, Rock
Llyn ............................... Lake
Llys ............................. Palace
                    Princes dwelling
Maen............................. Stone
Maes ...................... Open Field
Mawr ...................... Big, great
Melin ............................. Mill
Moel ......................... Bare hill
Morfa ..............Marsh, Seashore
Myn ....................... Ore, Mine
Mynachlog ................ Monastery
Mynydd..................... Mountain
Nant ................... Stream, Vale
Newydd ......................... New
Nos............................... Night
Pandy.................... Fulling Mill
Pant....................Hollow Valley
Parc............................... Park
Pen........................Head, End
Pentref.... Hamlet, End Settlement
Perfedd ........................ Middle
Plas ................... Hall, Mansion
Plwyf ........................... Parish
Pont............................. Bridge
Porth............................. Port
Pwll...............................Pool

13

| | |
|---|---|
| *Pistyll* | Waterfall |
| *Rhaeadr* | Waterfall |
| *Rhaglaw* | Government Officer |
| *Rhiw* | Hill |
| *Rhos* | Moor |
| *Rhyd* | Ford |
| *Rhyngyll* | Beadle |
| *Sarn* | Causeway |
| *Sir* | Shire |
| *Tir* | Land, Territory |
| *Traeth* | Beach, shore, stand |
| *Traws* | Cross, District |
| *Tref* | Township, Town |
| *Tŷ* | House |
| *Ty'n Llan* | Vicarage, Rectory |
| *Uchaf* | Upper |
| *Ynys* | Island |
| *Ysbyty* | Hospital |
| *Ystad* | Estate |

# Nefyn

## The history of Nefyn

Although much of the history of Nefyn and its surrounding area will become apparent from a perusal of the notes attached to the following walks, it may be of interest to give a general account of some of the aspects of Nefyn's history before setting out.

The origin of the name Nefyn may come from Naf 'lord' with the suffix '- yn'. According to Baring Gould, the old name was 'Llanfair yn Nefyn'.

The town of Nefyn has been an important place in Llŷn for many centuries, indeed, its importance greatly outweighed that of Pwllheli for most of those centuries. Nefyn was a seat of power in the 11th and 12th centuries for the Welsh Princes.

Not long after the victory of the Norman invasion under William I, at Hastings in 1066, Norman Barons were ensconced in proto-marcher lordships along the Welsh/English border. The main centres for these lordships were Chester, Shrewsbury and Hereford. This area, later to be called the March of Wales, was to act as a buffer to any Welsh action against England and also as a base for campaigns against the Welsh. Throughout the 11th and 12th centuries these Marcher lords made repeated forays into Welsh territory and brought large areas under their control, mainly in southern and central Wales. The classic Norman 'motte and bailey' castles were quickly erected in any district nominally brought under Norman control. North Wales and in particular the mountain fastness of the kingdom of Gwynedd proved a more daunting obstacle for Norman infiltration, but repeated attempts were made, mostly from the Chester lordship, and campaigns in 1090 and 1114 penetrated as far as Llŷn.

There are four earthwork 'castles' on Llŷn of the motte and bailey type, at Abersoch, Pwllheli, Bodegroes and here at Nefyn. (Next to St Davids church and behind the newly built toilets is the remains of a mound, now crowned by a watchtower built in connection with the herring fishery, this mound is the remains of the motte & bailey castle.) It is a debatable point whether these castles were Norman outposts or, as seems more likely, were constructed by the native Welsh, copying the Norman pattern. The North Wales Prince, Gruffudd ap Cynan certainly used the Nefyn castle as a base in the early 12th century for sea-borne activities in his struggle for ascendancy in Anglesey and Arfon. A motte and bailey castle consisted of a roughly circular low earth bank as an outer defence which would be topped by a wooden palisade. This enclosed area was called the courtyard or bailey. In this area were numerous wooden buildings, stables, kitchens, storehouses etc. In the centre of the bailey, or to one side, was an earth mound topped by a wooden tower, the keep or motte. This was the most strongly defended part of the castle. For speed of construction, when a new territory had been taken, the tower was made of wood, but when and if the castle became established it would have been replaced by a stone keep.

Nefyn was the administrative centre of the commote of Dinllaen (Llŷn Cantref was divided up into three regions called commotes [see fig 2], each with its administrative centre). These commotal centres were called 'maerdrefi'. A maerdref consisted of the lord's holding surrounded by a village of bondsmen — unfree peasants tied to the land and lord of the manor by work duties and tributes for the upkeep of the lord and his family. For example, most of the servile families had to give a proportion of any grain grown on their lands, and of butter and cheese produced from their own herds. Vegetables, honey, ale, beer, cider, and fish, also had to be handed over as tribute. Work duties included, fetching and carrying, repair of fences, buildings, hedges, roads, bridges, and the maintenance of mills and unblocking of streams. Certain days of the week had to be set aside for carrying, harrowing, harvesting and threshing for the Princes' farms. In the 12th and 13th centuries the number of bond cottages, the maerdref, was large, but there was a tendency for the freemen to increase and the number of bondsmen to decrease. This was due to two factors: firstly, as society gradually became more enlightened there was an increasing number of bondsmen allowed to earn their freedom, either by

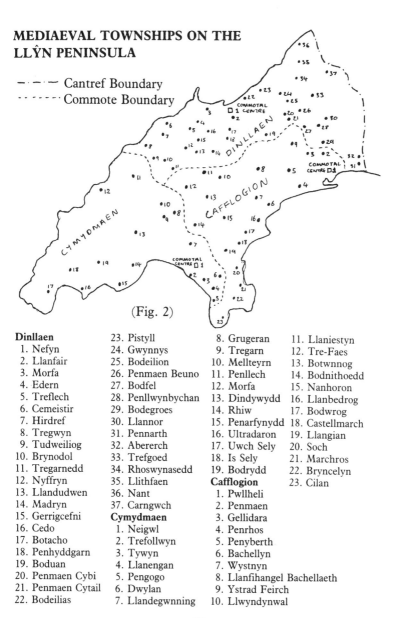

# MEDIAEVAL TOWNSHIPS ON THE LLŶN PENINSULA

--- Cantref Boundary
...... Commote Boundary

(Fig. 2)

**Dinllaen**
1. Nefyn
2. Llanfair
3. Morfa
4. Edern
5. Treflech
6. Cemeistir
7. Hirdref
8. Tregwyn
9. Tudweiliog
10. Brynodol
11. Tregarnedd
12. Nyffryn
13. Llandudwen
14. Madryn
15. Gerrigcefni
16. Cedo
17. Botacho
18. Penhyddgarn
19. Boduan
20. Penmaen Cybi
21. Penmaen Cytail
22. Bodeilias

23. Pistyll
24. Gwynnys
25. Bodeilion
26. Penmaen Beuno
27. Bodfel
28. Penllwynbychan
29. Bodegroes
30. Llannor
31. Pennarth
32. Abererch
33. Trefgoed
34. Rhoswynasedd
35. Llithfaen
36. Nant
37. Carngwch

**Cymydmaen**
1. Neigwl
2. Trefollwyn
3. Tywyn
4. Llanengan
5. Pengogo
6. Dwylan
7. Llandegwnning

8. Grugeran
9. Tregarn
10. Mellteyrn
11. Penllech
12. Morfa
13. Dindywydd
14. Rhiw
15. Penarfynydd
16. Ultradaron
17. Uwch Sely
18. Is Sely
19. Bodrydd

**Cafflogion**
1. Pwllheli
2. Penmaen
3. Gellidara
4. Penrhos
5. Penyberth
6. Bachellyn
7. Wystnyn
8. Llanfihangel Bachellaeth
9. Ystrad Feirch
10. Llwyndynwal

11. Llaniestyn
12. Tre-Faes
13. Botwnnog
14. Bodnithoedd
15. Nanhoron
16. Llanbedrog
17. Bodwrog
18. Castellmarch
19. Llangian
20. Soch
21. Marchros
22. Bryncelyn
23. Cilan

17

paying for it in cash or by some noteworthy deed. Secondly, during the 13th century Nefyn began to attract many free settlers from other areas, so that by 1284, when a survey of Dinllaen commote was done, the ancient maerdref of Nefyn consisted of only five households, this number was overshadowed by a community of fifty or so free households, described in the record as the *borough* of Nefyn. The occupiers of these households were the equivalent of the 'burgesses' of the English market towns. Along with these burgesses were a small and recently formed group of native free men called 'gwyr y farchnad' or 'market men'. Fairs and markets were a principle feature of commerce at this time. Baring Gould writes:

'Fairs were very generally held on the festivals of the church, and always it would appear on the festivals of the Welsh Saints, sometimes the fair was held on the eve of the Saints day. To take Nefyn for instance its old name in full was Llanfair yn Nefyn, with dedication to the Virgin on the feast of assumption. There were fairs on two of her eves O.S. March the 24th and August the 14th. This by the way puts the supposed dedication to Nefyn or Nyfain, daughter of Brychan, out of court.'

These regular fairs and markets brought Nefyn and Llŷn into contact with outside trade, and were underlining her dominant role in the area. Nefyn was also situated on the pilgrim route to Enlli (*Bardsey Island*) and much trade was doubtless done with them, as sometimes, large numbers of pilgrims would travel together often in a marked 'holiday atmosphere'. This trade of Nefyn was largely responsible for weaning the local tribal economy off the ancient exchange and barter system and onto a money economy. In concert with this idea many of the traditional dues and renders paid by the bond peasants were transmuted into cash payments. Nefyn was a prosperous and growing town, a survey conducted in 1293 showed that the population had doubled since 1284.

As a reflection of the growth and prosperity of Nefyn and Pwllheli, both towns were formally granted the status of a 'free borough' in 1349 by the Black Prince. The towns as well as other lands in the area were granted in the terms of this charter, to Nigel de Lorying or Loharen. Sir Nigel was a leading member of the Black Prince's household. Thomas Pennant who was a writer travelling in this area in the latter half of the eighteenth century says of Nefyn:

'This place had been bestowed upon Nigel de Lohareyn by the Black Prince in the 12th year of his Principality, and made a free borough, was allowed a guild mercatory, with every privilege attendant on other free boroughs, and all the Liberties and customs granted heretofore to that of Newborough in Anglesey. He also gave it a grant of two fairs annually, and a market on a Sunday, to which the inhabitants of that part of the commote of Llŷn, then called Dinthlayn were obliged to resort.'

The wording of part of the charter runs as follows:

'Greeting know ye that we with the will, and assent of our beloved and faithful Nigel de Lohareyn Knight, our Chamberlain, to whom we have lately gave and granted the towns of Nefyn and Pwllheli with the apportenacies in North Wales for the term of his life . . .'

This period of wealth and prosperity is abruptly curtailed in the year 1400. The name of Owain Glyndŵr is familiar to us all, of Welsh Princely descent with an English upbringing — he was at Oxford, studied law in London, spent time in the court of Richard II and campaigned as squire to Henry IV. Glyndŵr was responsible for the first truly Welsh nationalist uprising. This uprising was born of many factors, political, social and economic unrest, but there was also a resentment at the increasing degree of 'Englishness' of many of the boroughs, such as Nefyn. It was decided that the burgesses of Nefyn were far too amicably disposed towards the English and the town was completely destroyed and all the lands laid to waste in 1400. Almost 20 years later the town was still totally deserted and regarded as a ghost town of ill omen, indeed, it can be said that Nefyn never fully recovered from this disastrous blow. What recovery there was, was slow, and by the end of the 15th century the town was showing only a slight increase in population from the early years of re-settlement. The chronic shortage of population caused by the devastation in 1400, changed not only the course, but the character of Nefyn's history. With so much vacant land available, when repopulation commenced it was by burgesses from far flung areas. These new burgesses had been living in environments, socially and economically at variance with the previous conditions of Nefyn and so they brought new ideas with them. Thus, among other things, the locally traditional ideas of land ownership and the mechanism of its passing from one generation to another, or the way in which it was sold or otherwise changed hands, was gone forever.

Only during the sixteenth century with the general re-shaping of land owning structure and farming techniques, does recovery begin to gather some momentum. There was a tendency throughout the Tudor period for the formation of, initially, small estates, centred on the manor house. By 1600 most of the land in the Dinllaen commote surrounding Nefyn was divided up between different estates at the expense of the old traditional open field system. The largest and most influential of these estates near Nefyn were those of Cefnamlwch, Madryn, Bodfel and Boduan.

There was a crisis in Nefyn in the 1630's when the crown tried to reassert its ancient rights to certain lands in the area. The matter reached a flash point in 1632 when the king's Receiver-General, Humffrey Jones, visited Nefyn and confronted in the churchyard a body of burgesses opposed in the majority to the rent rise which would have accompanied any recognition of royal rights to local lands. The spokesman for this group of land owners was Thomas Wynne of the Boduan estate and a near riotous situation developed in the churchyard resulting in the hasty retreat of Humffrey Jones. There then follows a period of litigation-at-a-distance with the court of Exchequer Chamber in London. As implied earlier there was a small minority of burgesses in support of the royal rights, these were members of the Cefnamlwch estate. There had existed, since the rise of the Wynne family of Boduan, a mutual opposition between Boduan/Bodfel and Cefnamlwch that went back to their differing tribal origins. This dispute in 1632 added fuel to the fire of opposition with accusations of profiteering levelled at both factions. If the names present in the list of the members of the court-leet of Nefyn in the 17th and 18th centuries are compared, a shift in the balance of power in favour of the Wynnes can be detected.

The terms of the charter of 1349 granted the town of Nefyn a considerable degree of self government, under their own elected officials which comprised Mayor, Deputy Mayor, Recorder, Sergeant at Mace, Borough Constable and two Bailiffs. These officers were elected by the whole body of burgesses who were members of the court leet except the Mayor whose office was hereditary. The two bailiffs were to all intents and purposes tax collectors, town clerks, magistrates and general policemen rolled into one. There were two annual meetings of the court-leet; at Michaelmas when the election of officers took place and in May when a grand jury of burgesses made report to the bailiffs of any misdemeanours of the local populace. Offenders were imprisoned in the borough gaol. In addition to the two main meetings there were monthly meetings when necessary, to deal with minor matters such as debt and trespass.

The old town hall was the site of this former corporation court house. The following are some of the announcements and oaths taken by some of the officers appertaining to the court, taken from the Corporation Oath Book 1815: Sergeant of Mace:

'Oyes! Oyes! Oyes! All manner of persons that has any business to be done in this Court let him come forth and appear this day fortnight and they shall be heard. God save the King.'

Subpoena for witness — 'You are hereby required, all excuses apart, to be, and appear at the court to be holden and kept for the Borough of Nefyn on Saturday, the day of instant, to testify the truth of your knowledge in a case depending between AB Plaintiff and CD Defendant, in the plea of Trespass in the case, etc. on the Defendant (or Plaintiff) as the case may be, hereof fail not.'

Bailiffs Oath: (This oath was Sworn by Bardsey Bailiffs, it shows that Bardsey was dependent on Nefyn for at least some of its judicial procedure).

1st. 'You shall well and truly use Exercise and enjoy the Office of Bailiff for and with in this Lordship of Bardsey and Liberty during the time being.'

2nd. 'You shall be obedient to his Majesty that now is, his heirs and lawful successors King and Queens of England for ever.'

3rd. 'You shall justly and truly execute all such processes mandates and Warrants to you directed and delivered and then to return and deliver up according to the direction thereof without dread or malice.'

4th. 'You shall not Attach or Arrest the Body or Bodies, Goods Chattels nor Cattle, of any Person or persons without a prescript of Billet from the Recorder and Deputy Steward of this Lordship first had and Granted or his deputy in that behalf. So help you God.'

### The Oath of a Packer of Fish:

'You shall well and truly swear to execute the Office of a Packer of Fish within the Port of Portinllaen, in which you shall see what White and Red Herrings shall be packed in lawful Barrels and Vessels and shall be well truly and Justly laid and Packed and shall be of one saving or drying and equally well packed in every part of the Barrel or Vessel, and you shall also see that all Cod fish and other salted fish shall be packed in the said Port, shall be well truly and Justly packed, and you shall also see that everything belonging to the said Office of a Packer be well and truly executed within the Port aforesaid, according to the best of your skill and knowledge. So help you God.'

### Oath and Allegiance:

'I AB do sincerely promise and swear that I will be faithful and bear true allegiance to his Majesty King George. So help me God.'

### Oath of Supremacy:

'I AB do swear that I do from my Heart Abhor detest abjure as impious and heretical that damnable doctrine and Position that Princes excommunicated or deprived by the Pope or any authority of the see of Rome may be deposed or murdered by their subjects or any other whatsoever. And I do declare that no Foreign Prince, Person, Prelate or Potentate hath or ought to have any power,

Jurisdiction, Superiority, Preeminence or Authority, Ecclesiastical or Spiritual with this Realm. So help me God.'

**Oath to be taken by all Officers and Burgesses in Corporations:**
'I AB do declare that it is not lawful upon any pretance whatsoever to take arms against the King and I do abhor that Traitorous position of taking Arms by any Authority against his person, or against those that are commissioned by him. So help me God.'

**Directives to a Burgess:**
'1st. You shall be Obedient to his Majesty King George the Third, his Heirs and Lawful Successors of Great Britain for ever.
2nd. You shall also be obedient to the Mayor and Bailiffs of this Corporation in all lawful Command and them aid and Assist in the Execution of their Office to the utmost of your power.
3rd. You shall keep his Majesties peace in your own person and uphold observe and keep all ancient Orders laudable Customs and privileges of this Town.
4th. You shall not suffer any part of the Common Lands to be infringed or encroached upon by any person or persons to the utmost of your knowledge.
5th. You shall Aid and maintain the Liberties of this Town, and not bear with any foreign occupier or aid them against the Liberties of this Town.
6th. You shall contribute with the free men and Burgesses of this Town in all Taxes Lays and Assessments, for the King and common weal of this Town, where there unto required.
7th. You shall pitch and pay Scot and Lot and all Duties according to the ancient uses and customs, within this Town.
So help you God.'

A few more interesting instructions, guides and directives given to Corporation officials:
' 1. You must enquire if anyone save those in the Liberty, living in this town inclines to the Church of Rome rather than to the Church of England.

2. You must in the same manner enquire into every kind of treason against His Royal Highness King George III, and that such be presented to the Court, to be convicted according to the statute that was made for that purpose.

3. You must enquire into any case of murder or any unlawful act.

4. You must enquire if the Highway is in receipt of support for its repair according to the statute.

5. You must enquire if anyone is breaking the peace and law within the liberty of this Corporation or living antagonistically from the Christian religion, and that such be presented to the Court.

6. You must enquire that no one makes holes for the purpose of diverting water from the old road except without the Corporation boundary to the peril of his Majesty's subjects.

7. You must enquire that no one draws any commons to his house or land without licence from the court.

8. You must enquire if anyone in this town is keeping two kinds of scales or weights one to sell and the other to buy.

9. You must to the very best of your ability be unanimous in preserving the law in this town and Liberty of the corporation, and to the best of your knowledge be perfectly accurate in explaining all matters brought before you appertaining to the law in accordance with the oath taken by you.

10. You must search for a fit person to take the office of Bailiff for the town for the coming year.

11. You must enquire and see that no one tampers with the Pinfold without the authority of the Constable.

12. You must carefully observe that meat-dealers do not sell unwholesome meat.

13. You must see that all good rules are observed for the sake of his Majesty's peace, and to observe *keenly* that Bread is sold in conformity with the price of wheat, and that wheat, bran etc., is sold by correct measure or weight; and you will not suffer anyone to trespass in the way of narrowing His Majesty's Highways or Streets in this town by placing thereon refuse, or waste, broken glass, and middens etc. You must comport faithfully yourselves

(and observe that peace and honesty be maintained in this town and Borough).'

The vast majority of the cases heard by the Nefyn Court-leet were of debt or trespass, occasionally something a bit different crops up, for example: 'At the Court holden 8th Jan'y 1757 Margt Arthur Wido Plantif Declared that Owen Thos Deft Calld her a thief before two Sufft Witnesses that she the sd Margt Arthur had stolen Curtains from Madryn the House of Wm Bodvell Esq and sold the same to the Revd Mr. Owen Rect of Bodvean — 2sh for the Poor by agreement. Memorandum. That this Grand Jury opened a footway from Penisa'r Dre to Bwlch Abergelis through Jn Hugh's garden along the green border between Jobe's Quillets.'

*27th May 1758:*
. . . at this Court Wm Ellis presented the Wall of the Mill Dam being much out of repairs and the Tent., agreed to repair it out of Hand.

*29th September 1759:*
On the 12 Oct. pl. (plaintiff) declared that deft. (defendant) Jane Williams spoke something to her defame that she the pl. was naughty with Owen Hughes's son but leaves the particulars to the witnesses.

*7th Jan 1775:*
Mary Evans v Elizabeth Roberts plea of trespass on the case (six white penny loaves for the poor. Pl. declared that the Dft. did say publicly that she the said Mary Evans was a jade, bold and unreasonable in decoying other women's husbands that her husband had much ado to keep himself honest from her).

*5th July 1777:*
"Memorandum that this Grand Jury opened a Road from the Great Road to Edern at John Ellis' House along Rowland Mark's Quillet across Robt Jones' Quillet and Evan Jeffrey's Quillet to a Quillet

called Pant yr Orsedd" — (A 'quillet' is a small strip of land cultivated by one person, it may be isolated or be in a field alongside other quillets. It reflects the ancient mediaeval open-field system in which a communities agricultural activities took place in huge fields divided into strips each tended by separate people. The strips were divided by low banks, now hedges).

Through the many centuries of Nefyn's history no industry or activity has held more importance than fishing. (For those interested in a fuller description of the fishing industry in Nefyn and the rest of Wales we draw their attention to the excellent book, published in 1991, *The Inshore Fishermen of Wales* by J. Geraint Jenkins from which the following information is largely derived).

Although all forms of fishing such as for cod, lobsters, crabs etc. have taken place around Nefyn, nothing can rival the herring in importance; indeed, the sign depicting '3 herrings' is the symbol for Nefyn. Nefyn was an important herring port as long ago as 1287 when in a survey, 63 nets were found to be owned locally. Herring fishing was carried out at many ports on the Welsh coast, but Nefyn and Aberystwyth constantly vied for preeminence. There was a noted increase in the amount of in-shore fishing during the 16th century, this increase continued into the 17th century when George Owen wrote in 1607 concerning the huge shoals of herring around the coast:

. . . 'which being in great store and sold to parts beyond the sea, procureth also some store of money . . . This fishing is chiefly from August till neere Christmas, the middle or first fishinge is counted best as that which is fullest and fattest. The order of taking them is with drovers (that is, with nets which drift with the tide) and shootteings of nettes in known places chosen especially for the fairness of the ground, which nettes are shoote in the evening, the later the better, and drawn up in the morninge with such store of fishe as pleased God to send.'

The male population in the early and mid 17th century in Nefyn was around 60. Nearly all were employed in the herring fishing during its season. For the remainder of the year they would work on their farms, or at other crafts, but everything was dropped in the herring season.

An inventory from around 1680 shows this admirably:

Einion ap Adda — 9 oxen, 6 cows, 20 sheep, 3 heifers, 3 fishing nets
Ieuan ap Madog — 4 oxen, cow, horse, heifer, boat and 4 nets
Llywarch Crun — 1 cow, 1 net
Bleddyn Fychan — 6 oxen, 3 cows, 2 horses, 1 small boat, 3 nets
Tangwystl Wraig Addaf — 2 cows, horse, heifer (3 years old), 1 net
Dai Bach — 2 sheep, heifer, 2 nets

Herrings were caught in Caernarfon Bay and Cardigan Bay, but it was commonly accepted that those from Caernarfon Bay were much the superior, particularly those caught in the vicinity of Nefyn, for according to a traditional verse:

> Penwaig Nefyn, penwaig Nefyn,
> Bolia fel tafarnwyr,
> Cefna fel ffarmwrs.
>
> *Nefyn herrings, Nefyn herrings,*
> *Bellies like innkeepers,*
> *Backs like farmers.*

There seemes to be a bit of a slump in the fortunes of the Welsh herring fisheries in the first half of the 18th century, but this was rectified partly by *The Act for the Encouragement of the British White Herring Fishery* in 1750. Inshore fishing showed a marked increase in the area in the second half of the 18th century. Thomas Pennant writing about the area in the 1770's states:

'Notwithstanding the laudable example of the gentry, the country is in unimproved state, neglected for the sake of the herring-fishery.'

He goes on to say:

'The herrings, about the year 1771, were taken here in vast abundance, from *Porth Ysgadan*, or the *Port of Herrings*, to Enlli (*Bardsey Island*). The capture amounted usually to the value of about four thousand pounds. They were sometimes salted on shore; at other times bought from the fishers by the *Irish* wherries at sea, and carried to be cured in *Dublin*. These desultory fish, about the period mentioned, appeared in *July* and went away in *October*; in earlier times they came in *September* and went away in *November*.'

With respect to other types of fishing around Nefyn he says:

'*Dories* are often taken here. The fishermen were wont to fling them away, on account of their ugly appearance: nor was this luxury known to the gentry, till one of their servants, who was acquainted with the fish, informed them of its being an inhabitant of these seas. The *Atherine, Br. Zool iii No 157* (Zoological nomenclature before the introduction of the Binominal system of Linnaeus) is taken near *Pwllheli*; and a small lobster is often found burrowing in the sand; but differs from the common kind only in its place of residence, and in size. The traps for lobsters are made with pack-thread, like thief-nets, and baited with pieces of the *lesser spotted shark, Br. Zool iii No 47*. The fishers remark, that the sexes of these voracious fish consort, at times, apart; for at certain periods they take only males, at others only females.'

Let us allow Edmund Hyde-Hall to have his say, this, about 30 or so years after Pennant:

'Along this bay [Nefyn] are built the curing houses of the herrings, which are captured during the season in considerable numbers. Here also, under the Point, is a small pier for the protection of the fishing boats, of which about forty belong to this port. Each of these is commonly the joint property of seven persons, who out of the season are either agriculturists or tradesman or engaged in the coasters which supply the Liverpool market from this neighbourhood with poultry, shell-fish or other smaller articles. At the commencement, however, of the fishery, all other avocations cease, and every thought and wish is directed to the improvement of the advantages held out by these annual bounties of providence. Mr Pennant has expressed his opinion that the interests of agriculture suffered from this diversion of employment but in reply to my enquiries, which upon the account of that opinion were repeatedly and carefully made, I was satisfactorily assured that no injury whatever of the sort could accrue, inasmuch as the harvest was always either housed or at least saved before the coming of the fish. It is plain therefore that if no actual evil does exist, much benefit remains not only from the profits of the occupation, but from the increased supply of animal food.'

*Port of Nefyn with fishermans huts*

The herring shoals, as the 19th century advanced, became more and more sporadic, some years hardly any were to be caught, other years saw a glut. In one season so many herring were caught in Nefyn that they were dumped in huge rotting piles on the beach, and farmers from all over the district took them away by the cart-load to be spread on the field as fertiliser. In the leaner years some people attributed the lack to divine punishment for misuse of food in times of plenty. All the main herring ports of Wales e.g. Tenby, Milford Haven, Fishguard, Aberystwyth, Swansea etc., were experiencing very mixed fortunes towards the end of the 19th century with catches declining year-by-year. Nefyn had ceased to be a herring port of any significance by 1914. The bonanza was over, the vast shoals of herring were gone.

The fishing techniques used to catch the herring were basically the same in all ports, but each had its own variations and traditional methods. Nefyn had two main fishing grounds. One in the bay called Y Gamlas, the other Y Swangins. Although these inshore grounds were sufficient for local supplies the fishermen often ventured as far as the Irish Coast.

The boats used on Llŷn were widely differing in size and shape depending on the port in question. At Abersoch, for instance, with its shallow, safe, and sheltered beaches large boats of some 32-34 ft were used, whereas at Aberdaron where the sea was almost invariably rough, small boats around 14ft were favoured as these were deemed safer in heavy seas. At Nefyn the boats fell somewhere in between, around 18ft long and with a beam of 7ft. The Nefyn boats had one difference from the norm in other ports, they were double ended. These 'female boats' were not popular elsewhere, the square or rounded stern 'male boats' were preferred. The Nefyn boats were crewed by 3 or 4 men pulling the huge oars of 14ft or so, with one man steering, usually the owner of the boat. Each man had 2-3 nets. These nets were imported from Ireland and were of a fine mesh of around 1 inch and fitted with floats on the upper rope or *tant* and weights on the lower *tant*. They were in the region of 50 yards or 22 *gwrhyd*, a *gwrhyd* was (approximately 6 feet) long and between 6 and 10ft in depth. The weights consisted of stones with a groove or channel cut round them (a process called *nitsio*), the resulting grooved stone *poitshis* was then attached by a thin wool thread to the lower tant of the net — traditionally made of grass — every *gwrhyd*. The cork floats on the upper tant were roughly the same distance apart. One or two locally made anchors were used to hold the net in position. When the fishing ground had been reached, the anchor attached to one end of the net was dropped into the sea, the boat then moved away until the length of the net was in the sea, then the other end of the net was lowered. Depending on the fishing ground being used there would be a difference in the way the net was fished. At Y Gamlas an anchor was attached to both ends of the net so that it remained in a fixed position. In contrast, at Y Swangins only one end of the net was anchored, the other was allowed to pivot round in the tide. It was supported by a leather buoy *bongi* some 2ft across. This large buoy also acted as a marker. The catch was always equally shared out among the crew with one share being allocated to the boat.

The method used for counting out fish for the purposes of sale is highly antiquated. Herrings were always sold by the 'meise' (*mwys*) or a combination or fraction thereof. A meise consisted of five 'hundreds', a 'hundred' was actually 120. Two score of fish would be counted and one put aside as a tally, the 'warp', after five score another was put aside to mark a 'hundred' this was called the 'tale', so a 'meise', therefore consisted of 120 x 5 a 15 'warp' = 620.

Another method of counting a 'hundred' was to count three fish at a time, two in one hand and one in the other, this was repeated forty times to produce the 'hundred'.

The catch was processed in several ways. The fish could be sold fresh to merchants (*croeswrs*), who would then sell them to outlying farms, houses and villages, or, as in the early 20th century transport them by train to Liverpool.

If the fish were not to be sold fresh, as was the case when large numbers were caught, they could be treated in a number of different ways. One method was called 'bloatering'. In this process the fish were pickled in brine or dry salt for an initial nine days, then further salted in specially constructed salt houses for about three weeks. They were then washed and often subjected to a second salting period of a few days. The large quantity of salt used in this process was imported from Ireland. Quite often farmers would buy the herrings fresh and do the bloatering process themselves.

An alternative method of preserving herrings was by smoking. One technique was to smoke fish that had been split, cleaned, and lightly pickled before hand in special smoke houses, this method was called 'kippering'. A second smoking method was to smoke the fish whole after a longer pickling time, the smoking time was then longer. This process produced the 'Red' herring.

There is a legend attached to the fishing community of Nefyn:

One afternoon in September in the early 1700's a fisherman was out in the bay in his boat, his name was Pergrin. The fishing was slack and Pergrin was looking around when he thought he detected some movement inshore towards the cliffs, he rowed silently in this direction, and as he got closer he could see, sitting on a rock, a mermaid combing her long golden hair. So silent was Pergrin's approach, or so mesmerised was the mermaid by the vision of her own beauty reflected in her looking glass, that Pergrin was able to grab her and haul her into his boat. She thrashed around wildly and tried to escape, but Pergrin held on tightly! It was the biggest catch of his life. Folk tradition does not enlighten us on the language normally used by mermaids, but this one spoke fluent Welsh and she begged and pleaded for release. Pergrin was reluctant to let such a prize go but he was moved and softened by her tears. Finally she said:

'Pergrin, if you will let me go, I will give you three shouts in your hour of greatest need.'

Pergrin could resist her entreaties no longer and allowed her to dive over the side of his boat and with an elegant twist of her tail she was gone. Pergrin thought never to see her again. Then one hot, calm afternoon, Pergrin and a number of other fishermen were out in their boats, when suddenly he saw the head of the mermaid appear in the sea by his boat.

'Pergrin, Pergrin, Pergrin,' she cried urgently,

'Take up your nets and return to shore.'

Pergrin was much puzzled by this warning, for the day was fine and the sea was calm, but he instantly obeyed, pulled in his nets and hastily returned to shore. No sooner was he ashore when a terrible storm broke out, as if from nowhere. Eighteen other fishermen who had gone out were drowned.

To end this section on Nefyn's History, and to provide a little of the flavour of past times, we include here a few traders advertisements as they appeared in a guide book at the turn of the century.

## WALKS 1, 2, 3: NEFYN — GWYLWYR

Garn Boduan Circuit
Garn Boduan
—— Road
---- Footpath
(1), (2) etc numbers for
History notes

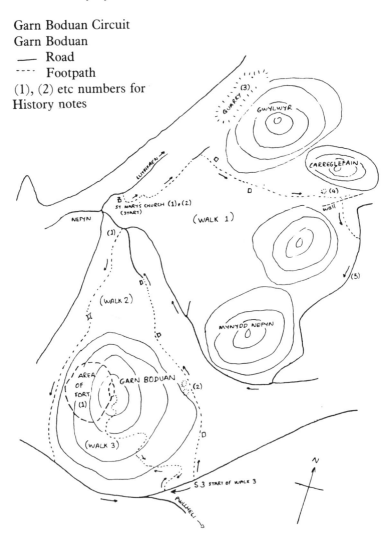

# Nefyn — Gwylwyr

2½ hours

*This walk although not difficult, takes you through areas of gorse so it is advisable to wear strong trousers and shoes. The going is fairly strenuous as you will be ascending hills, but paths are adhered to.*

Start from St Mary's Church [1] on Stryd y Mynach (*Monk Street*).

Set off on the path alongside the church beside a stream which will take you past a children's playground, turn left at the end of the playground. This playground is the site of the Priory in which Gerald of Wales possibly stayed during his visit to Nefyn.[2] You will now be heading in the direction of Mynydd Nefyn, keep to this path.

After a while the path joins a larger farm track where after about a 100 metres you will come to a wooden footpath sign at a kissing gate set in the wall, go through this, turning left and in a short distance passing a well (unnamed). Enter through another kissing gate and continue uphill.

On your left are emerging views over Porth Dinllaen.

Continue on past some cottages and over a small stream, the path then comes to a 'T' junction, your path leaves the road and heads uphill opposite the joining road — you will need to hunt around for the entrance to this path as it will be overgrown in the summer, it begins on your right just before the junction. Go up a few steps on a path with a handrail and through a small gate into a field, head uphill keeping to the wall on your right and heading towards a cottage, at the cottage the path crosses a stone step stile and leads behind the cottage through a walled path, at the end of this path, cross the field in front of you heading uphill in the direction of another kissing gate, about 150 metres. If you are under 7 stone in weight pass through the gate, everybody else over the wall.

At this point you may be interested in the Gwylwyr quarry and a short detour to your left will bring you into this.[3]

Head uphill towards the next cottage, passing through the wall just in front of it and over the next wall on a stone step stile. Follow this path towards the peak in front of you called Mynydd Carreglefain.

In a few hundred metres at the junction of three walls climb into the next field (containing the mountain), by way of a stone step stile set at the junction of the walls. Keeping the wall on your right, head uphill, passing the mountain on your left.

About 200 metres along the wall, opposite a stone step stile, the path you want veers to the left, follow this until the wall and path veer to the left. At the point where the path curves around in front of the wall, and about 100 metres from the cliff face, there is a reasonably well preserved stone hut circle — one of many in this area, although the rest are mostly ploughed out.[4]

In about 30 metres cross over the wall on another stone step stile, walk along towards the crags in front of you, after a short while this track crosses another set of tracks, but you carry straight on. After about a ¼ mile your track emerges onto a tarmac road, turn right onto this and continue.

After a while the views on your left will open out into quite a vista, with the broad sweep of the Llŷn coastline heading in one direction to St Tudwals Island and in the other across Snowdonia and onto 'Yr Eifl'.

Shortly you will pass on your right an old dilapidated cottage called 'Cerniog Uchaf', probably late 18th century. There are around here some fine examples of dry-stone walls.[5]

The road you are on has some gates along its length, please remember to shut them behind you. Passing through the last gate and onto the road, when in about 30 metres you will emerge onto a larger road, turn right and after a short distance you will see a well chosen picnic spot, because opposite this is a mediaeval site, (this site will be visited on the Garn Boduan walk), continue on this road until you arrive in Nefyn.

*Cerniog Uchaf*

*Nefyn Church*

# History notes

[1] Nefyn Church: The parish church of St Mary's consists of an undivided chancel and nave. There is a square tower at the west end. The porch on the north wall was added later, when the original entrance through a doorway in the west wall of the tower was converted into a window. The church was completely rebuilt around 1825 and the whole of its structure including its wooden fittings is contemporary with this rebuilding, further repairs took place in 1856. All openings have pointed heads. There is a circular recess in the west wall of the tower presumably for a clock and below this recess is a much eroded tablet bearing the date 1827. The belfry has an opening in each face and each corner of the parapet rises to a pinnacle.

The parish register of St Mary's church dates back to 1694. There is a decahedral stone font with a circular basin, probably mediaeval, standing on a modern base. There is a slate memorial tablet to Elin Wynn Saython, wife of John Parry of Nefyn 1679, and also a silver paten-cover with a London date-letter, also dated 1679 which was stolen in 1852. The present weather vane depicting a square rigged ship in full sail was renewed in 1962 but is a faithful reproduction of an earlier one, in its turn renewed around 1850. The present vane was made by the church warden of the time, John Hughes.

The church was held by the Augustinian Canons of Haughmond Abbey from the 12th century and a Prior of Nefyn is recorded in 1252. The fields to the south east of the church (now the playground) are called Bryn Mynach (*Monk Hill*) and Cae Mynach (*Monk Field*), these fields are possibly the site of the priory. This priory undoubtedly provided the hospitality for Gerald of Wales and Archbishop Baldwin in 1188, (see following note).

The church is now host to a thriving maritime museum, well worth a visit. The final Closure Service was held there on Thursday, 8th September, 1977.

The loquaciously observant peripatetic penman, Edmund Hyde-Hall observed the following when confronted with St Mary's church:

38

'The church is a plain small parallelogram pretty well kept. Upon the pulpit is the date of 1718, but without any explanatory inscription. Within the building is a monument to Elinor Wynne Saython . . . wife of J. Parry of Nefyn who died at the advanced age of 100 years in 1679. Here to is kept a school.'

[2] Giraldus Cambrensis or Gerald of Wales: Gerald de Barri was born in 1146, and spent his childhood at Manorbier Castle on the Pembrokeshire coast in South Wales. His father was a Norman Knight, William de Barri, whose family took its name from Barry Island, off the Glamorgan coast. His mother, Angharad, was half Welsh. As soon as age permitted, Gerald was sent to the Benedictine Abbey of St Peter in Gloucester where he was educated for a career in the church. Between 1165 and 1174 he was in Paris. When he returned to England and Wales he was granted ecclesiastical benefices in both countries. An Archdeacon of Brecon, named Jordan was reported by the zealous Gerald for living with a mistress, he was dismissed on the spot and the resulting vacancy was filled by Gerald. It was this title which he still held many years later in 1188 when he toured Wales with Archbishop Baldwin and wrote his famous book *The Journey through Wales*.

The purpose of this tour through Wales was to preach the cause of the Crusades, Gerald and the Archbishop would stop anywhere where there was a number of people, they would then preach to, harangue, and coerce people to 'take the cross' and go and fight against the Saracens in the Holy Land. Many people, on hearing their impassioned words would come forward from the crowd and enlist in the 'army of God' on the spot. This momentous journey, undertaken by Gerald and Archbishop Baldwin with a small entourage, commenced during the first week of March in 1188 from the border town of Hereford. The journey was to be a complete circum-navigation of the whole country of Wales. The main course of the circular route is as follows: From Hereford to New Radnor, then on to Brecon, south through Abergavenny to Newport and Cardiff, then along the south coast through Margam, Swansea, Kidwelly, Carmarthen, Whitland, Haverford West to St

Davids. After resting at St Davids the party started out along the coast northwards through St Dogmael's, then slightly inland to Lampeter and Strata Florida. After visiting the Abbey there, they journeyed back to the coast at Llanbadarn Fawr, on northwards through Tywyn and up to Cricieth. From there they cut across Llŷn to Nefyn where they arrived on the eve of Palm Sunday to receive hospitality at the Priory of St Mary. From Nefyn they proceeded along the North Wales coast passing through Bangor, Rhuddlan, Basingwerk and on to Chester. From Chester they struck southwards through the Welsh Marches down to Oswestry and then to Shrewsbury and then the final leg of the journey back to Hereford. The book *The Journey through Wales* and its companion volume *The Description of Wales*, which are available in modern translations, make fascinating reading as Gerald was a gifted writer, and this, coupled with an eye for detail in all the places and people that he encountered, presents the modern reader with an unparalleled picture of Mediaeval Wales.

When the travellers were at Nefyn, Gerald reports that he found a book for which he had been searching for years: *The Prophesies of Merlin*.

'There I myself, Archdeacon of St David's, discovered the works of Merlin Silvester, which I had long been looking for.'

The Merlin of the King Arthur legends, has evolved from an amalgamation of two different figures. One is this Merlin Silvester, of Scottish origin, the other is Myrddin Ambrosius or Myrddin Emrys (associated with the Dark Age hillfort of Dinas Emrys near Beddgelert). The magical and prophesying side of the Merlin of legend is mainly derived from 'Gerald's Merlin', Merlin Silvester.

[3] The Gwylwyr quarry was opened in the 1830's as a response to the increasing need for granite setts for durable road surfacing. By 1835 the quarry was in the hands of Samuel Holland who in 1844, succeeded in bringing together a few quarrying enterprises in the area as the 'Welsh Granite Company'. The quarried setts were lowered down the steep inclined track which can still be seen, and onto the beach, just under Wern caravan site, where they were loaded onto ships. Activity declined towards the latter end of the

19th century as demand for granite setts for road-working lessened in favour of macadam.

[4] The hut circle here is the remains of a homestead dating with all likelyhood from the Romano/British period circa 3rd-4th centuries A.D. It is typical of its kind in its circular stone construction and in being sited on upland pasture. It probably represents the pastoral holding of a single family. These round huts of the Romano/Celtic and Dark Age period were simple primitive structures but eminently functional and durable. Constructed as they were, of a low, thick stone wall with a conical thatched roof supported by slanting timbers, they were of the ideal geometrical configuration to shrug off the worst effects of wind and rain, to which their elevated and often exposed situations made them liable. There are quite a number of other comparable hut sites in this upland area and it seems that for a pastoral based farming community the well drained upland pastures were seen as superior to the coastal lowlands and valleys, it is certainly true in the Llŷn peninsula that the vast majority of farms of this period occupy elevated situations.

[5] The dry-stone walls seen here are fine examples of their art. Very tentatively, dry-stone walling was probably first practised on Llŷn, to any great extent that is, towards the end of the 16th century when the process of estate building began to be seen, with private landowners wishing to delineate their estate boundaries and set aside areas of land for different purposes. As the estates grew in size and complexity, throughout the 17th and 18th centuries, the frequency of such walling increased. Then, with the large scale enclosures of common land into these estates in the early years of the 19th century, the criss-crossing of the countryside with dry-stone walling became a feature of the landscape familiar to us all.

## Walk 2
# Garn Boduan Circuit

**2½ hours**

**This walk is along reasonably flat paths and skirts the hillside of Garn Boduan, the scenery is pretty and largely wooded.**

Set off from Stryd y Rhos at Capel Seion. Head out of town and in a few metres you will come across a house called Tan y Dderwen (*under the oak*). Bear right here, and across the road from the house you will see a footpath sign, carry on until the first kissing gate, go through this and keeping the fence on your left head towards the gap in the trees,[1] entering the next kissing gate on your right.

Keeping to the right hand side of the stream, make for another kissing gate which will be apparent after passing the single stone gate post, after the kissing gate cross the small stream on the foot bridge, following the footpath to the right, take the top or higher path.

Continue along this path, skirting the hillside, passing the remains of a kissing gate. Keep on this track for some distance until you are facing two gates, take the lower one and then the track emerges onto the main road where you will turn left.

Keep on this road until you see the sign for Y Ffôr, here you will turn off onto a less busy road, which is sheltered under a canopy of mixed trees (just before the brow of the hill is the starting point for walk 3 which will take you up the hill you are walking around).

Turn off into the 'Nantcol' stud-farm, following the track around. At the last gate, which is tied shut, climb over and head towards Mynydd Nefyn, which is the peak in front of you. Go through the field gate and head up the small valley towards a wall. If you look to your left, in a field just below the woods is a mediaeval site mentioned in the last walk.[2]

Set off from here crossing more field gates until you reach a small cottage. Bear left behind this until you cross a wooden stile and then you walk past the edge of the woods passing through a

*Flank of Garn Boduan
from the path*

*Woodland ride*

*Old Farm building at Fron Fawr*

pleasant woodland ride. At the end of this, enter the kissing gate in front of you and proceed downhill in the direction of Porth Dinllaen.

Keep descending passing through a field gate, keep the hedge on your right, then head into a walled lane and through the field gate at the end of this. Keep between the buildings of Fron Fawr and into another walled lane, passing an old chapel graveyard on your left, you are now back in Nefyn.

## History notes

[1] It is possible that the flat field at this point is the site of a mediaeval tournament. The final defeat of the Welsh forces by King Edward I occurred in January 1283. A year later as part of a victorious sojourn through Wales it was decided to hold a glorious tournament. This was to be a show of power and a reminder to the Welsh of their subjugation as well as a celebration of victory. Nearly all the 'important people' were present as were many noblemen from overseas.

> 'Where throngs of knights, and barons bold,
> In weeks of peace high triumphs hold.
> With store of ladies, whose bright eyes
> Reign influence, and judge the prize
> Of wit or arms, while both contend
> to win her grace, whom all commend.'

The delay, of about a year from the date of Edward's victory, before holding the tournament, was caused by Edward deciding to await the birth of his son, this occurred in March.

It was decided that, as Nefyn was regarded as a seat of Royal power, it would be the place to have the tournament. The name of the street which runs from the village centre past a field called Cae Iorwerth (*Edwards field*), is Stryd-y-plas (*Palace Street*) and it is conjectured that somewhere along this street was the site of a princely palace — this would have been a large timber and thatched hall-house. It is recorded that repairs were carried out to this building in 1306, and in any case it would have been the only fit

*Possible site of Edwards Tournament*

dwelling to receive a king, its close proximity to the fields here lends further credence to the latter being the site of the tournament. King Edward was keenly interested in the King Arthur legends, and the theme of this tournament was King Arthur and his knights of the round table. It may have been another example of a show of power to the Welsh that an English king should 'hi-jack' Welsh mythology, which King Arthur surely was.

A notable event was said to have taken place during the course of this tournament, nothing less than the discovery of King Arthur's crown! 'nearby' (Studies in Mediaeval history presented to F.M. Powicke 1948. pp 265-6 notes). This may have been just an attempt to bring a theatrical touch to the proceedings. Whether this wonderful find was real or not it does demonstrate, along with Gerald of Wales' discovery of the book of 'prophesies of Merlin' a couple of centuries earlier, (mentioned in the last walk) that there was a powerful traditional link with King Arthur and the Nefyn area. This, when considered alongside the new and convincing evidence which we examined in some detail in the companion volume to this, placing the battle of Camlan near Aberdaron, and the possibility that Ynys Enlli (*Bardsey*) is the Avalon of the legends, it begins to place King Arthur, or some of his activities at least, firmly on the peninsula.

*Early Medieval homestead*

[2] These two features are the remains of an ancient homestead, accurate dating is impossible but they could cautiously be assigned to the late Dark Ages or early Middle Ages. The site, which has a much later stone wall running through it, is of a small hut/house

built of stone within a small irregular enclosure. The other feature may also be the remains of a hut and enclosure or of an out-building. Around 200 metres to the north east of the site can be seen traces of field terracing and ancient field boundaries, these may be contemporary and connected with the homestead.

# PLAN OF HILLFORT ON GARN BODUAN

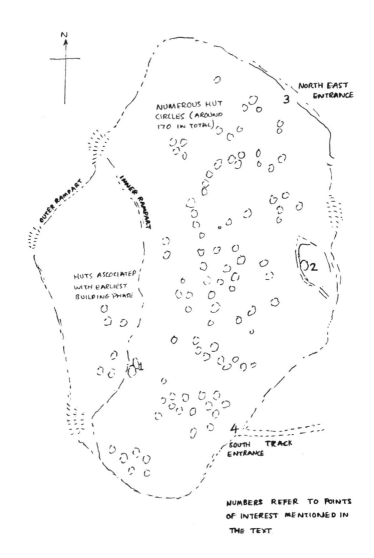

N

NORTH EAST ENTRANCE

NUMEROUS HUT CIRCLES (AROUND 170 IN TOTAL)

3

OUTER RAMPART

INNER RAMPART

HUTS ASSOCIATED WITH EARLIEST BUILDING PHASE

2

1

4

SOUTH TRACK ENTRANCE

NUMBERS REFER TO POINTS OF INTEREST MENTIONED IN THE TEXT

## Walk 3
# Garn Boduan

Refer to map for walks 1, 2, 3. Start this walk at 'S.3 start of walk 3'. This walk begins at the layby at the side of the main road at 'S.3'. Cross the wooden step stile and proceed up the wide stoney path. After a hundred metres or so this path swings sharp left and in a further 50 metres swings sharp right, but at this point another path leading off into the trees will be seen, this is the one to take. Follow this path as it winds its way up the hillside through the woods until it comes to the slightly steeper final slope up to the summit.

This hillfort (see plan) covers a very large area and encloses about 170 individual round huts in all. It is pre-Roman in date, (see note on hillfort building sequence in general) and along with Tre'r Ceiri and Garn Fadryn (both visited later in the book) forms possibly the earliest phase of fort building on Llŷn. These large stone walled forts differ greatly from the smaller, mainly earth-walled forts which came later, one or two of which are encountered and described in the companion volume to this work e.g. Pen-y-gaer, near Abersoch.

The construction work on Garn Boduan is of two phases, commencing, maybe around 300 B.C. The area enclosed by the earliest rampart rises from about 220 metres above O.D. on the west side of the mountain up to 300 metres. This early rampart is much damaged, it is better preserved on the north east side and can be seen to have been around 3 metres thick, there is no surviving entrance which can be demonstrated as contemporary with this phase and there appears to be only one hut which is demonstrably contemporary with this wall (No. 1 on plan).

The second phase wall is thought to have been constructed around 100 B.C. It is of similar construction to the earlier wall but is more impressive, being 4 to 5 metres thick and in a much better state of preservation, standing to a height of around 2 metres in places. On the south east side it generally follows the line of the earlier defence. On the west, however, it descends the hillside

*View from Garn Boduan*

*Part of Dark Age fortification on Garn Boduan*

somewhat, only six huts occur within the space enclosed between the earlier and later walls, it is possible that the extra space was used for the safe penning of live stock. With building in the second period, two entrances to the fort can be identified. That on the south east has been largely destroyed but seems to have been the most important as it was approached by a trackway. (No. 4 on plan). The other gateway is on the north east and is better preserved, due possibly to the fact that it had been blocked up in antiquity, it was a simple gap about 3 metres wide. (No. 3 on plan).

It would seem that the overwhelming majority of the stone hut circles were contemporary with the second period of construction. These huts occupy the largely flattish plateau-like area on the hill top, due to dense heather, very little is now discernible.

A probably more immediately rewarding area of the site for the casual visitor is the small and separate fort on the summit. (No. 2 on plan). It is separate not only in position but also in time, for this fort is datable, due to some finds of beads and pottery, to a period between the 2nd and 7th centuries A.D.

In its original form this small fort had two entrances, the one in the south remaining in use the longest, the western entrance was for some reason blocked.

The name Boduan translates into English as 'the abode of Buan'. Buan is said to have been a grandson of the famous 6th century Bardic poet Llywarch Hen, this would place Buan in the years c. 600 or 650 A.D. It is quite likely, therefore, that this small summit fort was the actual residence of Buan.

Returning for the moment to the subject of the large pre-Roman forts, it may prove interesting to give a brief general account of the background history of fort building on Llŷn.

Hillforts would have been the main settlement type in the Bronze and Iron Ages, but later development in the late pre-Roman, Roman and Dark Age periods would have seen a gradual, although not universal, abandonment of hillforts in favour of widespread, mainly upland non-nucleated (i.e. not arranged in a village structure) hut groups, holdings and farmsteads.

The first phases of building at the large stone forts of Boduan, Garn Fadryn and Tre'r Ceiri represent the first indication of large scale fortification. A conjectural date of around 300 B.C. has been assigned to this period. The resident culture in this area at that time was late Bronze Age in character. Why did these people suddenly find it necessary to spend such considerable energy on constructing these massive forts? It is thought that all this building was in response to the invasion of the area by Iron Age settlers, probably via the sea. After these hostilities were settled there are a couple of centuries of more or less peaceful co-existence between the two cultures. Around 100 B.C. a second wave of Iron Age settlers are thought to have arrived in the area and this sparked off the second phase of stone-walled fort building at Boduan, Fadryn and Tre'r Ceiri. The original Bronze Age culture, which may have still been in occupation of these three sites, rebuilt their fortifications in the same style as before. The earlier Iron Age people built forts of the earth-bank and ditch type or univalvate e.g. Pen-y-gaer. A third type of fort seen in Llŷn is the 'Bi-valvate' type with a double rampart structure, these are found mainly on the coast e.g. Dinllaen. These bi-valvate forts are probably associated with the second wave of Iron Age invaders.

# WALK 4: PISTYLL — PILGRIMS PATH

—— ROAD
- - - - FOOTPATH
(1), (2), etc NUMBERS FOR HISTORY
          NOTES

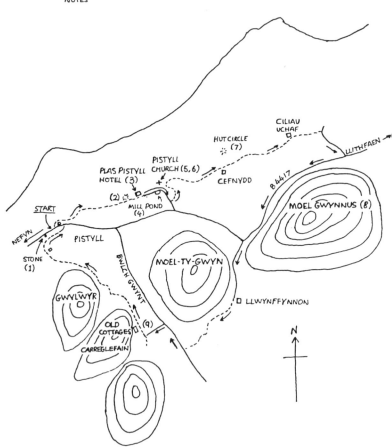

# Pistyll — Pilgrims Path

**3 hours**

*This walk is set in the parish of Pistyll, Edmund Hyde-Hall when visiting Pistyll in around 1810 had mixed views:*
*'That the political or agricultural or commercial value of this parish adds any great sum to the contributive powers of the country, none the most slightly acquainted with it will suppose, but abstracted from considerations like these, and viewed as a component part of the globe's great edifice, it must strike every spectator as an object full of interest, of sublimity, of horror.'*
*The walk is set amongst hills overlooking the sea, and the rest of the peninsula, in a remote area, the going is mostly easy although there are one or two sections that although never leave the path, climb quite steeply, but only for a short distance.*

This walk starts at the layby, map reference 322418 on the Pistyll/Nefyn road.

Before the actual walk begins it may be interesting to look at a stone[1] that marked the way for the pilgrims in their pilgrimage to Bardsey.

Head back down the road towards Nefyn and in about 100 metres on your left, in a wall and protected by a lintel, can be seen the ancient inscribed stone.

The walk proper starts at the footpath immediately in front of the cottage called Tŷ Isaf (*Lower house*) where you will see a footpath sign pointing in the direction of the coast. (The walk from this point follows the actual course of the Pilgrims route [in reverse] on this stage of their pilgrimage to Bardsey.)

Enter the small gate on the righthand side of the lane and head along the field border keeping to the fence, at the end of this field cross a wooden stile, turning right immediately and crossing a stone step stile, at this stile cut across the field heading towards the sea following an old grass covered field boundary and ditch.

After about 100 metres turn right and head towards an old white cottage in front of some crags, after a short distance you will come across a stile, cross this and continue along the rather unclear path.[2]

Opposite this cottage cross the stile and continuing along the path make towards the lane in front of the cottage, on this lane turn right and in about 20 metres turn left off the path over a stone step stile, on your left is the now poorly preserved Plas Pistyll (*Place of the spout or cataract*)[3]. Carry on down the left edge of the field through a large kissing gate. Keep on this path until it joins with a larger track where you will bear right, cross the old stone bridge and pass the mill pond,[4] which is quite an elaborate affair. Opposite this pond is the church at Pistyll.[4] [5]

*Mill Pond*

*Pistyll Church*

Coming from the church and returning to the road, turn left heading uphill towards the main road, turn left, where after a few metres you will see the footpath sign at a stile on your left which will take you off the beaten track and on to farm and heathland. After crossing the stile follow the field boundary and at the end of this you will meet a track heading uphill towards the ridge in front of you and bearing left up to the top of the ridge. At the top, go through the field gate and keeping the fence on your right continue along this track, after a while cross a stone step stile and head towards the farm house Cefnydd, after passing this, cross over the wooden stile and continue, keeping the fence on your right. In this field, on the far side, are the remains of two hut circles.[7]

Cross the next stile and head towards the main peak in front of you and in a while as you come over the crest of a hill a farm will come into view and just to the right of this is a stile, climb this and make towards the farm which is called Ciliau Uchaf. Just in front of it there is a green lane, go into this and follow it in front of the main building and through what looks like the garden, go through the gate and head uphill towards the main road.

Turn right at the road and continue on this for about a mile. At the big bend in the road you will see a footpath sign leading off across a cattle grid, continue along this track next to the mountain on your left, called Moel Gwynnys[8] until just before a cottage called Llwynffynnon you will see a footpath sign pointing over a stile, after crossing this turn left and head uphill towards the left hand upper corner of the field. There you will see another stile, after crossing this, keeping your back to the stile, head uphill following the line of the wall, at the end of the wall next to a heap of stones bear right uphill through a gap on the right of the drystone wall. Continue uphill following the wall and fence, after some 200 metres you will see a stile in the corner of the field cross this and head along between two walls along a green lane, at the end of this turn right and head towards the farm in front of you Tŷ Gwyn, cross over the wooden stile and pass the farmhouse on the left, go through the swing gate and emerge after 50 metres on to a larger lane, turn right here and turn left off the road at the farms called Tan y clogwyn and Penrhos. Follow the path past the cottage, make for the field gate, go through this gate and turn right, pass a pair of derelict cottages[9] following the path and keeping to the wall on your right. At the end of this path climb the stile and continue to the next gate, this time keep the wall on your left, after the gate proceed along this track past the cottage and then bearing right on the track heading downhill. On your left here are excellent views over Porth Dinllaen.

Continue through the next gate still heading downhill after a couple of hundred metres go through the last gate and emerge onto the main road turn left and in 100 metres you will see your car.

## History notes

[1] Stone: Eddie Kenrick, a local man who produced guide books for the area in the 1930's and 40's (see note on Edern village) says that this stone was a 'sun worshippers stone' and on it can be seen faint traces of a circle, cross and chains. The circle denoted the sun, and

the chains immortal life. In other words it is a pagan religious relic. This is somewhat at variance with the more commonly accepted view that it was placed here by monks on pilgrimage to Ynys Enlli (*Bardsey*) or marks the boundary of church land. According to the Royal Commission on Ancient Monuments the engraving on the stone is of a cross with bifurcated arms about 6in long projecting beyond a rough circle. Former local residents say that it was removed around 1860 from a position about 30 metres further south in a field called Cae Pen-y-Maer (*field of the head of the stone*). It may be 8th to 9th century in date. It seems logical to go along with the theory that the stone was placed here by monks on Pilgrimage as this road, which passes through Bangor and Caernarfon then Clynnog Fawr, past Yr Eifl down through Nefyn and on along the coast to Aberdaron, is the course of the route taken by monks fleeing from the monastery at Bangor Iscoed near Chester, when in 622 A.D., it was sacked by Saxons. Most of the monks were killed. The object of flight for the few survivors was sanctuary on the Isle of Bardsey and the monastery which had been established there in c.516 A.D. by St Cadfan. Throughout the following centuries such was the sanctity of Bardsey that three pilgrimages there were seen as the equivalent of one to Rome.

[2] The remains of this hut circle acted as an agricultural calender in the past. The changing position of the shadows cast by the stones in this 'circle' served as an indication of the seasons for sowing, reaping etc. Its later function, less edifying though probably no less socially significant, was as a cockfighting pit!

[3] Plas Pistyll: At the time the authors undertook this walk in June, 1994, this building was in a deplorable condition, but was undergoing repair. As a nice little example of history repeating itself consider Hyde-Hall's impression:

' . . . Plas Pistyll, was probably always a poor building, and is now in a very neglected condition.'

This observation was made in 1810 and is a description of an older building superseded by the present one. To continue with Hyde-Hall's description of the former house:

'A tall chimney rises from its gable end, and makes by its height a figure in the lone and dreary spot where it stands. Here, however, if I am not misinformed, is allowed, if demanded, to every passenger a meal, provided under the directions of an ancient custom. It may easily be supposed that this hospitable provision is not very frequently called for, if it actually exists. For myself, I was totally unacquainted with any such custom when I visited the place; nor did the tenant mention it, though he hospitably invited me to take what refreshment the house afforded.

[4] Mill Pond: The walled pond which is fed by a stream, was the power source of a mill during the last century. The mill building has now disappeared.

[5] Of all the churches on the Llŷn peninsula none evokes such an atmosphere of the ancient Celtic Church as this. In its remote sea-edge setting and with its simple appearance, it harks back to the period of the Celtic saints of the 5th, 6th and 7th centuries.

The church is dedicated to St Beuno who was the most important saint in North Wales. He founded a monastery at Clynnog Fawr in 616 A.D. He was supposed to have had miraculous healing powers.

During renovation of the church in 1949 the then rector, the Rev. Thomas Michaeliones, discovered a mural painted on plaster made from beet fat and lime with an inscription resembling 'Alleluia' in Gothic type lettering and 'DDL' in Roman numerals 1050 A.D.

The fabric of the west end of the church may be of the late 12th century, that of the east end is 15th century. The two south windows and the east window are modern. The west door is 15th century.

The font is noteworthy, it is probably of the late 12th century. The circular base is modern. The symbolic inscription on the font depicts 'Life without beginning or ending' and compares with Buddhist symbols used on ancient prayer wheels.

In the *Valuation of Norwich* c. 1254, a hamlet in the vicinity of the church is noted, called *Pistibus*. This hamlet and its surrounding area was a noted 'bed and breakfast' stopping place

*St Beuno's*

for pilgrims. As well as in the houses of the hamlets they could be accommodated at the nearby monastery, at the inn, or at a hospice on Cefnydd hill just to the north east, which we will be passing shortly. Here there is a field of some 20 acres in extent called Cae Hospice (*hospital field*) where there would have been numerous huts for pilgrims accommodation, rest and medical aid. There is also another field called Cae Hospice Pennla, this may be where lepers were catered for.

In the north wall overlooking the altar, is a leper window where they would stand, outside the church, to receive the sacrament. In the original building there was also a stone ledge for the 'aged and afflicted'. There is a tradition that the burial site of St Beuno himself is beneath the altar in this church.

The original building contained only two windows, one of which was the already mentioned lepers window. This early church was built of wood, plaster and thatch. The first stone building is probably 11th or 12th century. The roof was thatched until about 150 years ago and rope holes in some of the roof timbers can still be seen where the thatch was tied down to prevent wind damage.

Since 1969 the church has been regularly decorated with wild herbs, moss, flowers and greenery with rushes strewn on the floor, the effect of this when they are fresh is enchanting.

Rupert Davies (the actor who played Maigret) was buried here in 1976. During his life he donated funds for the upkeep of the church.

About 150 metres east-south-east of the church is a Holy well. It is covered by a concrete slab and is without visible ancient features. Water from this well is still used for present day baptisms.

[6] St Beuno: A few interesting, though no doubt apocryphal facts, emerge from hagiographical material compiled on St Beuno decades or even centuries after his death. For example:

When Beuno was resident at his principal church at Clynnog, he used to preach regularly at Llanddwyn. On one occasion he dropped his book of sermons whilst walking on the shore and it was swept away in the tide. After diligent searching he later found the book which was being guarded by a curlew. He immediately knelt down and prayed to God for a blessing on the curlew. God granted this wish and blessed the curlew with a nest which was hard to find.

In an exploit to help his niece Gwenffrewi or Winifred he shows a more formidable character:

Caradog, the son of a chieftain, attempted to force his attentions on Winifred who resisted stoutly and fled to one of Beuno's churches. She was pursued by Caradog and again repulsed him. Upon this Caradog drew his sword and cut her head off. A well gushed forth on a small hill where the head fell. The head rolled gently downhill to the church and the congregation being somewhat surprised to see a severed head roll in at the door, went outside to find the murderer cleaning his sword on the grass. Beuno upon arriving at the scene instantly cursed Caradog who died on the spot and disappeared from sight. The saint then picked up the severed head of Winifred and reunited it with her body, he covered her with his mantle and returned to the church to say mass. The girl rose up as if from sleep with a white thread-like circle round her neck. Winifred later sent Beuno a cloak, placing it on a stone near the shore, the sea took it from Holywell around to Llŷn, where Beuno found it, perfectly dry.

[7] The remains visible here are of a homestead of the Dark Age period. Any degree of close dating of such a dwelling is impossible, due to the fact that no datable evidence has been found in association with any comparable hut complex. On this point it should be said that virtually no excavations have taken place in this area on any hut group outside of a large fort.

*View from pilgrims path looking towards Nefyn*

In this vicinity are the fields 'Cae Hospice' and 'Cae Hospice Pennla' but we have been unable to ascertain the precise location.

[8] The large bare hill on the left is called Moel Gwynnys and the large farm on its north eastern slope is known by the same name. There are also two other farms within a ¼ mile or so which bear the names Foel Gwynnys and Cefn Gwynnys. Gwynnys is the name of a mediaeval township attached to the manor of Nefyn.

A township was, in mediaeval time, an administrative division of the land, it should not be thought of as a town in the modern sense.

It would have consisted of a loosely connected number of farmsteads and cottages spread over an area with more or less clear boundaries. The people living in such a township would fall into one of two main categories; free or bond. The bond tenant was totally tied to the soil, he was 'owned' by the lord of the manor, most of his work was done for the lord, indeed the cottage where he dwelt, with its small parcel of land was occupied by him only in respect of the work which he did for the lord. The bondsman was not allowed to move from the area, buy or sell anything (even if he had the money!), get married or anything else for that matter without the permission of the lord. The free peasant had things a lot better, technically he had freedom of movement, freedom to practice a craft from his own land for his own profit. Due to the natural strictures of mediaeval society this freedom was often more theoretical than practical.

The name Gwynnys may be derived from that of a Dark Age ruler, the common name Gwyn 'fair, white, blessed', compounded with the suffix — 'us' to donate the area under his control. The original form of this name may have been more like Guuness with the suffix 'i' meaning 'the territory of Guuness'.

There is more conjecture on the name Guunness. It brings into the story the early 5th century British leader Vortigern (Gwrtheyrn) and his connections with this area. (We will have more to say about Vortigern in the notes on the next walk.)

Nennius was a historian living in the 8th century, he collected together work by earlier historians and published the whole under the name *Historia Brittonum*. Over 20 chapters of this work are devoted to the attempts by Vortigern to construct a stronghold in the mountains of Hereri (Eryri/*Snowdonia*) in Guined (*Gwynedd*). He is based at the time at Dinas Emrys hillfort near Beddgelert with Ambrosius (Emrys Wledig/*Merlin* of the Arthur legends). Vortigern repeatedly fails to establish a stronghold and the reasons are explained to him by Emrys who advises him to look further afield for a site for a secure fortress. This he does leaving Dinas Emrys to Emrys (from whom it acquires its name). The text reads:

'And he gave him the citadel together with all the kingdoms of the western side of Britain, and he himself with his magicians proceeded to the northern side, and arrived at the region which is called Guunnessi, and there he built a fortress, which is called by his name Cair Guorthigirn.'

In the early years of this century a historian writes:

'Now there is a Gwnnws in the land of Llŷn, the name remaining yet on the slopes of the wild mountains of Yr Eifl. There too, is the deep inaccessible valley called to this day Nant Gwrtheyrn, that is, The Valley or Vortigern. And there, too, you may still see what are reckoned to be the foundations of his castle, and the green mound under which his ashes are believed to be buried.'

More recently the noted Celtic scholar Rachel Bromwich says:

'A variant tradition may have localised Gwtheyrn's end at Nant Gwrtheyrn in Llŷn, i.e. in the same district as Dinas Emrys. Perhaps this is the Cair Gwrthigirn of the Nennian list of Civitates which Nennius tells us . . . . was situated in *regio Guunnessi*, wherever this may be.'

It would seem from some rather involved place name evidence that the townships of Gwynnys had a subservient 'satellite' township in the nearby parish of Ceidio. Some of the ancient land records, if followed through the centuries show a connection despite considerable scribal error and natural evolution of word form.

> 1350/1 de hameletto de Roswethenassa
> 1352 Keydio e Ros Veinassaf
> Edw. IV Ros Wenessaf
> c.1550 Gunneth (Gunnes) habot otherwise
>       Rose Venessaph
> 1564 'vill' Rossevenasaph
> 1577 'vill' Rosse Venassaph
> 1598 Keido and Rose Venassaphe
> 1765 Rhos Gunnis

This 'Ros Veinassaf', 'Ros Wenessaf', 'Rosse Venassaph' etc is a compound of Rhos *moor* and Gwynysaf (Gwynnys Isaf, *lower Gwynnys*), and is thought to have been situated in the parish of Ceidio next to that of Nefyn.

The upshot of this evidence is that it would seem that the inhabitants of Ceidio had summer pasture rights on one of the 'Hafodau' of Moel Gwynnys. Briefly, this transhumance of livestock, as it is called, is the practice of keeping animals in the lowland areas near the 'hendre' *old or home farm/original dwelling, etc* during the winter months but pasturing them in traditional areas of high ground during the summer. Sometimes these high summer pastures would be at some distance from the hendre so that whole communities — or at least the members of which were involved with the animal husbandry — would live in the mountains in temporary dwellings for the summer. This practice of transhumance can be traced back into pre-history at least as far as the Bronze Age. It still continues in Welsh farming practice to the present day, but with modern transport allowing the farmer to return to his farmhouse. 'Hendre' and 'Hafod' elements are frequently encountered in Welsh place names.

The farmhouse of Gwynnys was once the seat of a gentry family. During the 18th century the family adopted the name of its home as its surname (Gunnis). This practice was common among the gentry *Uchelwyr* of Caernarfonshire e.g. Bodfel, Bodwrda, Madryn etc., are all family names taken from the names of their dwellings. There is a stone tablet in the house inscribed:

LL/HS/R(?)MAS/YEAR OF OrLORD 1719

[9] Cottages: It can be seen that the right hand cottage of this pair is very small. In fact these two cottage illustrate part of a developmental sequence in vernacular architecture of the 18th and 19th centuries. The simplest and, by inference, the earliest form of peasant dwelling was a small single roomed, open roofed cottage, sometimes without chimney or even windows. These cottages would be constructed of mud mixed with straw and with a thatched roof. In areas such as this where mountain scree boulders are readily to hand they would be used in the building. The next development in the typological sequence in peasant cottages, and demonstrated in the cottage 'next door' is the 'croglofft'. The croglofft cottage was not necessarily any larger than the single room type, although they often were. The croglofft was a second

floor in the cottage but covering only half the area of the floor space. Access to it was from a wooden ladder from the room downstairs. This 'half floor' upper storey provided valuable extra space and was often used as the bedroom. The next progression in the development is the logical one of extending the upper floor over the whole area of the cottage to produce a proper two storey house. The three types in the series do not necessarily form a chronological development, with one form supplanting the other, but all three forms were being built at the same time within the community, at least until the latter half of the 19th century.

# WALK 5: YR EIFL CIRCULAR

—— ROAD

- - - - FOOTPATH

(1), (2), etc NUMBERS FOR HISTORY
NOTES

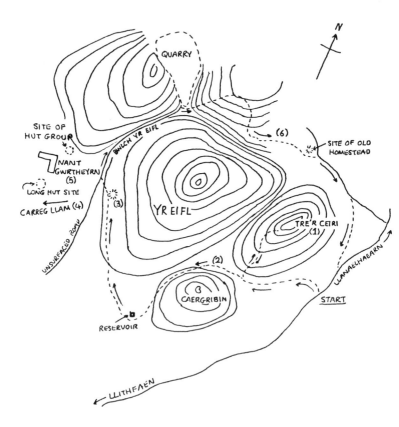

## Walk 5
# Yr Eifl Circular

**3 hours**

*The walk to the summit of Tre'r Ceiri is on very steep ground, and will tax the lungs of those who are not used to walking steep gradients. Approaching the summit is also very rocky and care should be taken here as there are a lot of loose stones. The walk to the summit only, is very short. The rest of the walk is over hilly, rough ground in places, but the views are well worth the effort.*

Start this walk at the layby on the Nefyn-Caernarfon road just before Llanaelhaearn and after Pistyll, the map reference is: SH 34/44-379 443.

Follow the footpath sign through the kissing gate, and heading uphill passing through on the way another gate, continue on up the slope over the wooden stile and follow the path to the left. At the fork in the path the right hand path leads you onto the summit of Tre'r Ceiri and into the ancient fort itself,[1] the other continues our walk around the mountain. After you have detoured to the fort retrace your steps to the fork in the path, take the other one this time and follow the path which will lead you, in a couple of hundred metres, towards a wall.[2] At the upper end of this wall is a stile, cross this and follow the path towards the gap in the peaks.

As you come over the brow of the hill you will meet with superb views over the whole of the Llŷn peninsula from coast to coast. The rocky arm of Porth Dinllaen reaching out into the Irish sea on your right, and across to the St Tudwal's Islands on your left. The peaks of Llŷn parade in front of you from Gwylwyr and Carreglefain at Nefyn to Mynydd Mawr at the far end of the peninsula at Uwchmynydd. All the other hillforts are visible from here so the people who lived here certainly had commanding views of the area.

At a wooden stile cross and bear left downhill, past a covered reservoir and in 30 metres take a path which takes you to the right

*View of Mynydd Carnguwch from flank of Yr Eifl*

*Nant Gwrtheyrn*

and towards the long ridge in front of you. The path you are on is not very well defined and crosses some which are much clearer, however, continue doggedly on over the ridge ignoring all other cross paths. After reaching the top, start the descent down the other side heading in the direction of the coast and making towards a gap in the hills down in the direction of the sea.

After several hundred metres you will meet up with a sizable track turn right on this — just over the summit of the ridge and before you meet the main track is an ancient sheep fold[3]. At this point on the track if you face the sea, the hill on your left called Carreg Llam (*rock of the leap*) used to be topped with a hillfort until recent years.[4]

The valley in front of you is Nant Gwrtheyrn (*Vortigerns Valley*).[5]

On your right in the distance is Holyhead, Anglesey.

You are now walking uphill, continue on this lane over the brow of the hill and then take the path to the left which is outside of the quarry fence leading in the direction of the coast. The village in front of you is Trefor, complete with its own mini pier. Descend in the direction of Trefor, following the ridge.

After descending for some time you will come to a drystone wall, turn right and follow it downhill, at the corner of the wall bear right towards a small gate in another wall at the valley bottom.[6]

Go through this gate, and keeping the fence on your left continue along this path, heading in the general direction of the large peak in front of you Gyrn Goch. Ignore the small gate on the left, this is a path which leads into Trefor. Make your way up to the small gate on the hill in front of you and keep on this path with the wall on your left. Just before the woods, the field you are now in is called Pant y Diogi (*hollow of laziness*). Cross the stile, and make your way through the woods (very dark) and after a hundred metres, out into the light, immediately crossing a stile emerging onto a tarmac road. The field in front of you as you climb the stile is called the 'field of the ruin' and is probably a reference to the old homestead the other side of the fence and visible from the stile.

Turn right on this road and follow it for about 2/5ths of a mile, at the footpath sign go through the kissing gate, following the path

*View of Gyrn Goch*

along an old grass covered wall, there is no well defined path here, but head diagonally up the hillside, cross the stile in the fence in front of you and follow the series of stiles until the last kissing gate through onto the main road, turn right and in 100 metres meet up with the layby and your car.

## History notes

[1] The hillfort on the inland peak of Yr Eifl is singularly the most impressive historic site on Llŷn, indeed, of its type, it is perhaps the most impressive in Northern Europe. At least it made an impression on Thomas Pennant, a late 18th century traveller:

'Across this hollow, from one summit of the Eifl to the other, extends an immense rampart of stones, or perhaps the ruins of a wall, which effectually blocked up the pass. On the Eifl is the most perfect and magnificent, as well as the most artfully constructed Celtic post I ever beheld. It is called Tre'r Ceiri. This, which was the accessible side, is defended by three walls; the lowest is very

# PLAN OF TRE'R CEIRI

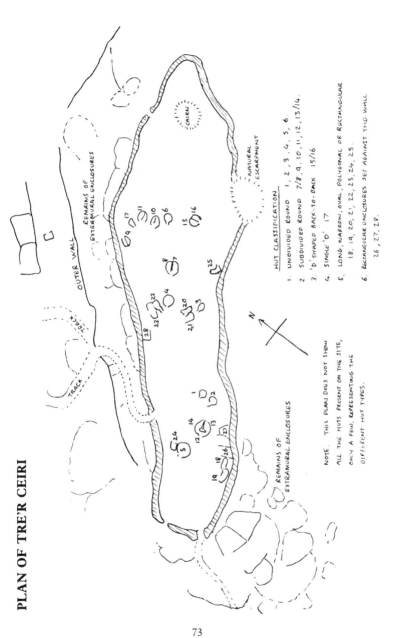

NOTE. THIS PLAN DOES NOT SHOW
ALL THE HUTS PRESENT ON THE SITE,
ONLY A FEW, REPRESENTING THE
DIFFERENT HUT TYPES.

HUT CLASSIFICATION

1. UNDIVIDED ROUND    1, 2, 3, 4, 5, 6.
2. SUBDIVIDED ROUND   7/8, 9, 10, 11, 12, 13/14.
3. 'D SHAPED BACK-TO-BACK   15/16
4. SINGLE 'D'   17
5. LONG, NARROW, OVAL, POLYGONAL OR RECTANGULAR
   18, 19, 20, 21, 22, 23, 24, 25.
6. RECTANGULAR ENCLOSURES SET AGAINST THE WALL
   26, 27, 28.

REMAINS OF
EXTRAMURAL ENCLOSURES

OUTER WALL

TRACK

REMAINS OF
EXTRAMURAL ENCLOSURES

CAIRN

NATURAL
ESCARPMENT

N

imperfect, the next tolerably entire, and has in it the grand entrance. This wall in one part points upwards towards the third wall, which runs round the edges of the top of the hill: the second wall unites with the first, which runs into a point, reverts, and joins the highest, in a place where the hill becomes inaccessible. The facings on the two upper walls are very entire, especially that of the uppermost. They are lofty and exhibit from below a grand and extensive front. The space on the top is an irregular area; part is steep, part flat: in most parts covered with heath, giving shelter to a few red grouse. The whole is almost filled with cells. To be seen to advantage, the station should be taken from the summit, about which the cells are very distinct, and disposed with much art. About the middle is a square place fenced with stones; a sort of *praetorium*, surrounded with two rows of cells; numbers are also scattered about the plain, and others again are contiguous to the wall along the inside.'

'The cells are mostly perfect; of various forms; round, oval, oblong, square. Some of the round were fifteen feet in diameter; of the oblong, thirty feet in length, with long entrances regularly faced with stone. All of them, when inhabited, were well protected from the weather by roofs of thatch or sod.'

'The upper wall was in many places fifteen feet high on the outside, and often sixteen feet broad. It consisted of two parallel and contiguous parts, one higher than the other, serving as a parapet to the lower, which seemed to have had its walk, like that on the walls of *Chester*. There was in one place a cell in the thickness of the wall, or perhaps a sally-port, in part stopped by the falling-in of the stones.'

So inspired was Pennant with this place that he begins his next paragraph:

'I was determined to trace every species of fortress of this nature which lay in the neighbourhood.'

Tre'r Ceiri was built probably around the same time as phase 1 at Garn Boduan and Garn Fadryn i.e. c.300 B.C. (For general account of fort building in Llŷn see notes on Walk No. 3 'Garn Boduan').

The area which is enclosed by the irregular stone wall forms a rough oval shape 300 metres by 100 metres approx (see plan). On this site are some 150 huts of various types. The main wall follows the natural line presented by the crown and brow of the hill. In its present state it varies between 2 and 5 metres in thickness on the north west side and 2 to 3 metres on the south and east sides. The best preserved sections are on the north and west and stand up over 4 metres on the outer face, and 2 metres on the inner face with a parapet occupying about half the thickness of the wall in places and rising to about 1 metre above the top of the wall. This has the effect of producing an inner wall-walk which would have been ideal for look-out work, and at times of discord in the area was doubtless patrolled at all times. There are a number of points of access to this wall-walk in the form of sloping stone ramps, still others may have been made of wood. It is probable that the wall-walk originally went round the entire fort. An outer wall extends from about 30 metres from the main wall on the north west side round to the northern end of the fort, at which point it is about 60 metres from the main wall.

This wall may be of a later construction than the main and can be seen as an additional defence on the side of the fort which has the easiest natural approach. It does not appear, from excavation, to have extended beyond its present limits and there was no parapet. The area delineated between the two ramparts contain a number of what are termed 'extra-mural enclosures', they are roughly circular in shape but very irregular. It is conjectured that some of these may have been cattle pens, and others garden plots.

A similar outer rampart occurs on either side of the approach to the south west gate.

In the last couple of years much reconstruction and repair work as well as excavations have been carried out at Tre'r Ceiri, under the aegis of the Gwynedd Archaelological Trust, notably on the north west gateway; Pennants 'grand entrance'. This gateway is approached by a trackway which commences about 50 metres outside the outer rampart, passing through a straight sided gap in this and then continuing at an angle across the slope to approach the main entrance.

The south west entrance is similarly approached by a trackway beginning beyond an outer rampart and then winding its way up the hill between a close concentration of extra-mural compounds in its approach to the south west main entrance.

In addition to these two main entrances there are three small passages through the inner wall on the east, west, and north. Only the latter has a corresponding entrance in the outer rampart, some 50 metres beyond which occurs a spring, undoubtedly a source of water for the inhabitants. This small north entrance in the main wall now appears impressive as it has had its lintel re-erected.

The highest part of the interior of the fort, on the northern end is occupied by the remains of a Bronze Age burial cairn which pre-dates the fort. Maybe its depleted state is due to having some of its material used in the construction of the fort. It is now a flattened mound some 12 metres by 15 metres in diameter. Recent excavation has demonstrated that as well as containing a primary cremation burial, other later cremations were interred in the periphery of the cairn after its completion.

The main enclosure of the fort is occupied by the numerous huts and hut complexes (see plan) which, as stated before, number around 150. Some of these are in an impressive state of preservation and some have been extensively re-constructed. The result is a superb archaelological site where it is easy for the visitor to conjure up a mental impression of a bustling Celtic fortified 'town'. (There is a useful information board on the track approaching the south west gate, for the benefit of visitors.

The huts present within the main enclosure, vary greatly in size and form, but due to their generally good state of preservation they can be arranged in a typological sequence (see plan).

1. Undivided round 1,2,3,4,5,6.
2. Subdivided round 7/8,9,10,11,12,13/14.
3. 'D' shaped back-to-back 15/16.
4. Single'D' 17.
5. Long narrow, oval, polygonal or rectangular 18,19,20,21,22,23,24,25.

6. Rectangular enclosures set against the wall 26,27,28.

The round huts range from 2 metres to 4 metres in diameter. (The average being between 2 to 3 metres. The typological sequence, 1-5 in the above list has also been shown by excavation to correspond roughly with a chronological sequence.

*Fine example of a round hut*

Tre'r Ceiri was built at the tail-end of the Bronze Age, occupied throughout the Iron Age and on into the Roman period. (During recent reconstruction of the north west gateway by the Gwynedd Archaeological Trust some Roman pottery was discovered). During the Roman period there is evidence that the climate was somewhat warmer that at present and Tre'r Ceiri was probably permanently and extensively populated. In former periods it may not have always been permanently occupied. It may have been used as a summer settlement or 'hafod' whereby it would be occupied by those people involved in looking after livestock brought to the high pastures during the summer months. It is evident, though, that its extensive and complex structure bespeaks a more important function than merely a temporary dwelling for shepherds and cattle herders. It must be admitted that in view of the potentially large number of people who could have occupied the site at any one time, their means of subsistence is problematical. We have evidence of cattle husbandry — the extra-mural enclosures, and it would seem that cattle raising was the basis of their subsistence. There is as yet, no direct evidence of any cereal growing. It is possible that in times of peace the site was occupied only minimally, with most people preferring to live in separate homesteads at a slightly lower elevation. In times of conflict the fort would be home to the whole tribe. It may be that the fort became permanently occupied for a long period in response to the presence of the 23rd Legion of the Roman army based at Segontium (Caernarfon), or alternatively it may have been instigated by the Romans themselves in their attempt to confine the native population into strictly defined 'reservation' areas, it is also possible that the same thing was occurring simultaneously at Garn Boduan and Garn Fadryn.

At any rate, after the Romans left at the beginning of the 5th century, the main bulk of the population abandoned Tre'r Ceiri and returned to their individual farms, but continued to use the fort as a summer 'hafod' settlement.

2 Whilst you are walking through this high pass towards Nant Gwrtheyrn pause a while and consider the reflections made by a gentleman correspondent to the 'Archaeloligica Cambrensis' (a periodical devoted to Welsh history and Archaeology). In 1864 in a long letter entitled 'A Day's Ramble About the Rivals' he writes, after having visited Tre'r Ceiri and following the route you are now on:

'The traveller next makes straight to the sea across the southern side of the middle hill, still at a considerable height, leaving on the left the diminutive church of Carnguwch and the slopes of Llithfaen where formally a string of hardy women might be seen very early in the morning pursuing their weary way to Pwllheli with necks bent under a load of heather for fuel, a few pence being the reward of their toil. Before long you approach the sea, and find yourself on the verge of a singular depression, or clear opening towards the water. This is no other than Nant Gwrtheyrn, which, in its quiet seclusion might well have furnished Dr Johnson with his idea of the Happy Valley in Rasselas, when sojourning with Mrs Thrale at her mansion of Bodvil, in this neighbourhood. A narrow road threads zig zag down the ride to the bottom, which is watered by a brook, and is diversified with meadows and enclosed fields. At the end next the sea is seen a mount with remains, which designated abode as Bedd Gwrtheyrn did the interment of the *carnfradwr*, or arrant traitor, as the Triads call him, for his invitation to the Saxons to uphold his usurpation. Besides an old tenement, a well-built farmhouse and offices may be seen. Former tenants were noted for their singularity. The greatest celebrity was a dwarf of hideous aspect with a large head, grinning teeth, squint eyes, small bandy legs, whose name was the bugbear of naughty children . . . If the glen is too deep to visit, you continue your walks along the ridge above the sea until you reach Carregyllam, a projecting rock of majestic height and outline, over whose brow none would venture to look down without a friend to hold him by the coat-laps. You are satisfied with rolling down a stone to dislodge the cormorants and seagulls from the inaccessible ledges below.'

Despite the rain of stones of possibly avalanchian proportions, unleashed throughout the 1860's on the unfortunate bird life by this worthy lover of wildlife, it appears that a few did survive as multitudes of their descendants still use Carreg y Llam today as a breeding ground.

[3] Sheep fold or hut circle? Sometimes, without excavation it is almost impossible to differentiate. Some small circular sheep folds are indistinguishable from round huts and indeed very many huts have been labelled 'sheep fold' on older maps. On the large-scale O.S. map of this area done over thirty years ago this is a 'sheep fold'. If it is a hut site it is a nicely preserved one and would repay excavation for verification.

[4] There used to stand on the top of Carreg y Llam the remains of a

*Sheep fold or homestead?*

hillfort. It was one of the few in Caernarfonshire which was positively datable to the post-Roman Dark Ages. The finds made during excavation included pebbles and boulders of varying size carried from the beach, two small worked-stone balls, and a few fragments of pottery around 8th-9th century date. This excavation was carried out on behalf of the Royal Commission on Ancient and Historical Monuments in 1954. This important archaelogical site is yet another to succumb, silently and without fuss, to the relentless march of commerce and industrialism. It was totally destroyed by quarrying in 1960.

The defences of this fort consisted of two dry-stone walls. The inner wall enclosed an area of oval shape 32 metres on the north-south axis, by 13 metres. The wall was 4 metres wide of rubble faced with masonry. The second wall stood about 10 metres outside this and was of slighter construction but with large blocks in its outer face. 16 metres to the south was a third rampart. North of the fort a wall extended to the north-west and enclosed a triangular area with the sea cliff as its west boundary. The enclosure shows remains of a hut dwelling. This was roughly circular about 6 to 7 metres in diameter, with an entrance on the south-west. It looks as though this was the only dwelling on the site. Access to the fort was gained by a trackway leading from the south east up to the simple gate set in the outer east rampart. The approach led from this gate to a second in the inner rampart.

[5] Nant Gwrtheyrn: For many years Nant Gwrtheyrn was known as a 'deserted village'. A few years ago work was begun, one house at a time as funds allowed, to convert it into the now highly successful Welsh language and culture centre. This village was built for the miners of the nearby Yr Eifl quarry.

There is in the valley evidence of much earlier settlement than of the mining village. The most readily visible evidence of this when looking down into the valley is the ancient field systems of possibly mediaeval — Elizabethan origin, delineated by dry-stone walling in the foreground, inland of the village. On the north east slope of the valley is the remains of a still more ancient settlement. It is of an enclosed hut group comprising three huts and associated enclosures contained within one all encompassing wall. This settlement is probably of early Dark Age date — 4th, 5th or 6th centuries. There is reference to a ruined chapel in a field adjacent to this hut group.

On top of a broad shelf at 250 metres on the opposite side of the valley are more remains of hut settlements. This time of rectangular long-huts. They are positioned roughly in a line of south east to north west axis and vary in length from 3 metres to 8 metres and in breadth from 2 to 4 metres. The remains of these huts are very difficult to see nowadays due mainly to a thick overgrowth of heather but it seems there were around 12 with other associated enclosures. It is tempting to think of this string of long-huts as a small village. A nucleated community of this type is far from usual in Llŷn where huts occur singly or at most in groups of two or three distributed fairly evenly over the higher ground. The accurate dating of these numerous hut settlements is impossible, although it is generally accepted that the round type were the norm throughout the Roman period and into the mid-Dark Ages, say 7th to 8th century, without datable finds from excavation it is impossible to narrow this margin any further. It is also generally conceded that the rectangular long huts are later in date than the round huts, say, anywhere between the 8th and 11th centuries. Obviously, there are only remains visible today, of huts, round or rectangular, that were of stone construction. Before, during and after the dates conjectured for them there were doubtless timber buildings, maybe only intended as temporary, and leaving no visible trace.

Nant Gwrtheyrn is first heard of as a village in a reference in the *Record of Caernarvon* in the 13th century. There was a dispute over land being heard by John de la Pole, Justiciar for North Wales. Evidence given by Ednyfed Lwyd, 'Nant Arthlythuaen' was mentioned by him as a hamlet granted by Llywelyn to one, Heilyn ap Tudur before 1282. These names occur again as *Nant Gorthern, Nant Gorthryen, & Llythvaen* (Llithfaen), *Nant e Lythvaen*.

The Elizabethan geographer and writer Leland called it 'Vortigers Valley' and 'Vallis Vortegerni'. After mention of Clynnog and Llanaelhaearn, he goes on to say:

'The nex paroch onto it on the shore is Egluis Epistil, wher cummith downe owt of a rokkie a litle rylle as it were renning yn a pipe. This rok is caullid Guotheren, i.e. Vallis Vortegerni in Llene.'

Mention of this valley and its legendary association with Vortigern has already been made in Walk No. 4,[8]. So who was Vortigern? Vortigern was a leader of the British people in the days before Arthur. With the passing of the Roman legions the Brythonic people — who after over 400 years of Roman rule considered themselves to be Roman — were in political turmoil. They were beset by barbarian hordes from the West by the Irish, and from the North, over the Scottish border, by the Picts. Around the year 424 a leader rose to power in the Gloucester area and soon established himself, precariously, as 'overlord' of southern Britain. Vortigern is not stricly speaking a name, nor yet is it a title, it means 'overking' or such like. It was the kind of name which fits only one man, in much the same way as 'The Old Man' meant Churchill and no one else and 'The Duke' meant Wellington and no other.

Vortigern was having a great deal of trouble defending his kingdom from the advances of the Picts and Irish, and thought he saw a solution. At this time the southern and eastern shores of Britain were subject to sporadic raiding by small bands of Saxons. These Saxons were usually in groups aboard one, two or three ships or 'keels'. Vortigern had the notion to enlist a number of these Saxons as mercenaries, to be paid to help the British see off the attacks of the barbarians. Hengist and Horsa, traditionally seen as brothers, and their three keels of warriors were duly invited ashore for negotiations with the Brythons. The deal was agreed upon and the plan seemed to work. In the process of repelling the Picts and Irish, many more Saxons had landed and were welcomed into the mercenary army under Hengist and Horsa, the numbers swelled until a considerable Scandinavian force was in Britain. With the threat of the Picts and Irish now receded, Vortigern was left to deal with this large Saxon army which had begun to realise that the land they were in was ideal for their purposes and that the British forces were weak, they were disinclined to leave. Vortigern had dug himself a hole. Inevitably, war soon ensued between the Brythons and Saxons. At some stages it seemed that peace was possible, as in the time when Vortigern married a daughter of Hengist, but it was not to be. Then came a time when a banquet was arranged for most of the numbers of both sides with a view to finalising a peace treaty. It was customary at that time that no arms were to be worn to a banquet, unless you were planning treachery that is! which is precisely what was in the minds of the Saxons. Each warrior had a concealed dagger and at a gesture from Hengist each Saxon stabbed the Brython seated next to him. All were slain except Vortigern. This event is remembered in history at 'the Treachery of the Long Knives'. As a result of these events Vortigern was suddenly seen by the Brythons as a traitor, firstly for inviting enemy armies into Britain, and then conspiring with them at a later date to get rid of many British nobles (present at the banquet) who may have been in a position to challenge his power. In the face of the rising fury, he fled for his life pursued by forces under the control of Emrys Wledig or Ambrosius (the same Emrys that Vortigern had given Dinas Emrys hillfort to) and a certain Germanus, a 'warrior bishop' from the continent. Vortigern fled north and west and was finally brought to bay here in this valley. He built himself a wooden stronghold, but the forces of Ambrosius were too strong, the citadel was fired and Vortigern was slain. Before his death, however, Vortigern was able to secure the escape of his daughter and grandson, they were taken to safety in a nearby large hillfort. The daughter's name was Madryn, her son's Ceidio. The hillfort is known as Garn Fadryn to this day and a parish with a boundary which runs to its feet is called Ceidio.

Almost inevitably our erstwhile travelling scribes Edmund Hyde-Hall and Thomas Pennant visited Nant Gwrtheyrn, so let them have their say. Firstly Hyde-Hall:

'But Nant Gwyrthern, [sic] or Vortigern's Valley, . . . . seems to be the chief object of that curiosity which loves to connect itself with former times. Dark and deep and horrid, it offers indeed a retreat at once calculated to elude notice and to supply the means of defence. Hither then Vortigern, flying alike from his Saxon foes and exasperated subjects, is said to have repaired; but to this wretched prince so many places of refuge from man, and of final punishment by Heaven's lightning, have been attributed, that all of them can scarcely have been properly so. The evidence, coupled with tradition, in favour of this place is supposed to rest upon the discovery of the bones of a large sized man in a grave said to be still dimly visibly. A tumulus or mound obviously for a sea defence to the valley may also be seen, but the place altogether appears calculated to repel rather than to invite a visit. Resentment might indeed force its way to the dark recesses, but the cupidity of war and of a warlike chief might easily be diverted to more profitable objects of adventure.'

Thomas Pennant: 'Ascend from Nefyn for a considerable way up the side of the side of the high hill; and after a short ride on level ground quit our horses, in order to visit Nant Gwrtheyrn, the immense hollow to which Vortigern is reported to have fled from the rage of his subjects, and where it was said that he and his castle were consumed with lightning . . . His life had been profligate; the monks therefore were determined that he should not die the common death of all men, and accordingly made him perish with signal marks of the vengeance of Heaven. Fancy cannot frame a place more fit for a retreat from the knowledge of mankind, or better calculated to inspire confidence of security from any pursuit. Embosomed in a lofty mountain, on two sides bounded by stony steeps, on which no vegetables appear but the blasted heath and stunted gorse; the third side exhibits a most tremendous front of black precipice, with the loftiest peak of the mountain Eifl soaring above; and the only opening to this secluded spot is towards the sea, a northern aspect! where that chilling wind exerts all its fury, and half freezes, during winter, the few inhabitants. The glen is tenanted by three families, who raise oats, and keep a few cattle, sheep, and goats; but seem to have great difficulty getting their little produce to market.'

'Just above the sea is a high and verdant mount, natural; but the top and sides worked by art; the first flatted; the sides marked with eight prominent ribs from top to bottom. On this might have been the residence of the unfortunate prince; of which, time has destroyed every other vestige. Till the beginning of the last century, a tumulus, of stone within, and externally covered with turf, was to be seen here; it was known by the name of *Bedd Gwrtheyrn*: tradition having regularly delivered down the report of this having been the place of his interment. The inhabitants of the parish, perhaps instigated by their then minister, Mr Hugh Roberts, a person of curiosity, dug into the carn, and found in it a stone coffin, containing the bones of a tall man. This gives a degree of credibility to the tradition, especialy as no other bones were found near the carn; nor were there any other *tumuli* on the spot: which affords a proof at least of respect to the rank of the person, and that the place was deserted after the death of the royal fugitive, about the year 456.'

Apart from the Vortigern legend, there is another locally famous legend connected with Nant Gwrtheyrn. The story, the culmination of which takes place in the 17th century spans many centuries. It begins in the time when there were monks living in the vicinity of Beuno's shrine. It came to the attention of the monks that the inhabitants of Nant Gwrtheyrn were pagans and it was decided that three of the brethren should go to the village and preach the gospel. The men of the village, however, would have none of Christianity and drove the monks away with curses and stones. Then came the monks' turn for cursing, when at the head of the valley they turned and looked down on the heathen village at its bottom and, proclaimed their own curses. No one who was born in the village, spoke one monk, should ever lie in consecrated ground after death. Another said, no male or female born in the village should ever be able to marry each other. In the fullness of time the village would decay and die, to become a deserted ruin, declared the third monk.

It seemed that the first two of these curses was effective. Over generations the men of Nant Gwrtheyrn who were mainly fishermen were drowned, either at sea in storms or falling from cliffs. Their bodies were never recovered and no holy ground received their bones. The women also suffered fates that precluded burial in sacred ground. The inhabitants of the village, in time, were converted to Christianity but the curses remained in force. Men and women both, being mindful of the second curse, always sought to marry someone from out of the village.

Sometime during the 17th century when memory of the curses was becoming a thing of the distant past, a man and a woman of the village fell in love and decided to marry. All seemed to be going well right up to the day of the wedding which dawned bright and fair, the bride and groom, as was customary, exchanged presents on their wedding-morning, the bride's present to her man was a puppy. Following another old tradition, the bride hid herself in feigned bashfulness, and it was the duty of the friends of the groom to search her out and carry her to the church. But when the ritual search was enacted the girl could not be found, they searched for hours, throughout the day and on into the night, still she was missing. The following day the whole village went out to look for the missing bride, the search continued for many days throughout the whole area, but she was never found. The bridegroom, distracted with grief, spent all his time wandering the sea strand clutching the small dog that had been his wedding gift. Some villagers discovered that the dog was dead, still in his arms. It was taken from him and its body cast into the sea. The memory of the terrible tragedy cast its pall over the village for many years. Generations later there came a night of a violent storm, thunder and lightning crashed down around the cliffs and the small village huddled between them. The following morning when it was calm again, the villagers went around to survey the damage caused by the storm. One huge oak tree with a hollow interior growing near the houses had been split by a bolt of lightning, and, in the gap created, the astonished people beheld a grisly sight, a skeleton, gripped as in a vice, and on its head long hairs of gold, and it wore a wedding dress of purest white.

The skeleton was placed with reverence in a coffin and was harnessed to a horse to drag it up the steep road and so to St Beuno's church for burial. Upon reaching the top of the cliffs the horse stumbled and fell down the precipice, the coffin was smashed to matchwood and the bones were lost among the boulders so that none could be recovered for burial in consecrated ground.

As the years passed, roads and quarries opened in the area and life and prosperity came to Nant Gwrtheyrn, a new village was built for the miners, with gardens, fine cottages, a school and a chapel, no one paid any attention to old curses and legends. But the curse of the third monk was not be be denied, the quarries closed, the miners left, the village died, the cottage windows gazed like black sightless eyes into the north wind.

In recent years life has once again returned to the village in the glen. Do the sonorous words of the monks curse of all those centuries ago still echo around the valley of Nant Gwrtheyrn?

[6] As we crossed the top of Bwlch yr Eifl between the two peaks and near the quarry we crossed a parish boundary — from Pistyll into Llanaelhaearn. Technically speaking we also left the Llŷn

peninsula. As we descended the ridge down into the valley we passed into lands which were once part of a mediaeval district or township. In fact two townships lay next to each other here. The valley through which we are passing belonged to the township of Hendre Fawr. The township of Elernion ('Aelhaearns land' in district of Llanaelhaearn 'Aelhaearn's church') occupied a strip of land beginning just inland from the modern village of Trefor stretching towards Llanaelhaearn. (The wooded area corresponds roughly with it.)

In an area such as this many layers of human influence on the landscape can be detected. Early settlement and agricultural patterns being overlaid by later ones, but, in a rural environment such as this, not quite being obliterated. It may be interesting to describe briefly an outline evolutionary sequence of settlement type which would have been typical of this part of Wales.

The Neolithic period would have seen the first permanent settlement in the area, they were the first farmers, and this method of subsistence made it possible to remain in one locality more or less permanently, as opposed to previous societies which had an enforced nomadic or semi-nomadic existence as, being hunters, they were obliged to move with the game on which they depended. Very little evidence has come to light of any dwellings or other structures attributable to this period except the enigmatic standing stones of which North Wales abounds.

Likewise the Bronze Age which followed the Neolithic. Although the end of the Bronze Age may have been witness to the first fortified large-scale hillfort settlements e.g. Garn Fadryn, Tre'r Ceiri and Garn Boduan (all three described elsewhere in this book).

It is with the coming of the Celts in the Iron Age that we begin to see a more widespread pattern of permanent farming settlement. We see many more hillforts along with isolated huts and small enclosed hut-groups.

The advent of the Roman period, and their ensuing four centuries plus of political control, saw a hiatus in native settlement evolution. With the demise of the Romans and their subsequent withdrawal, this evolutionary process could begin anew. Set against a backdrop of political turmoil, tribal chieftains and their folk tried to carve out and establish territories of their own. Such a chieftain would first establish a hendref (*old settlement*). This hendref would be the nucleus of the tribal gwely (*resting place*). The gwely was the extent of the arable land which the chieftain had been able to bring under his influence. Once this land had become established as belonging to this tribe, and, if the chief had sons — as he invariably did — the land would be divided equally between these sons according to the ancient Welsh custom of *gavelkind*. The land thus divided was known as rhandir (*shareland*). A principal drawback to the system of partibility of gavelkind was that, as the generations passed and the number of sons increased, the land of the gwely became more and more divided into parcels of ever-decreasing size down to and beyond an economically viable limit. This could lead to expansion of the gwely beyond its original boundaries, or, if this were not possible due to other surrounding and competing gwelyau or the surrounding land being infertile or such-like, then friction, competition, and hostilities could easily develop between landholders. Within the gwely the other alternative of course, was warfare with neighbouring gwelyau. After around 1100 A.D. a large gwely or a group of smaller ones would be officially designated as a 'township'. The dwellings within such a township tended not to be grouped close together or 'nucleated' but spread out, each tyddyn (*homestead*) belonging to an individual clansman. By the 14th century the typical tyddyn settlement comprised around 10 acres of land distributed through several sharelands. It was an 'open-field' system of agriculture, with large fields divided into strips (*lleiniau*) separated by narrow strips of unploughed land. Each individual farmer would not own consecutive strips to form a block of land, but would own several strips in widely scattered areas.

This illogical-seeming system of having small bits of land spread all over the place, in time, gave way to the gradual accumulation by each tyddyn of more localised blocks of land. This process was achieved by farmers in numerous ways e.g. swapping land with a neighbour, purchase, coercion, force etc. This development was largely complete by the 16th century to produce a series of compact agricultural units, small farms, larger farms and small estates with hedges or walled fields. This process continued with estate owners becoming more powerful and expanding their holdings at the expense of smaller less powerful ones. This continued until they were rich enough and possessing enough political clout to enforce the enclosure of vast areas of common lands to enable their estates to become ever larger and richer. This forced small farmers and cottagers during the late 18th to early 19th centuries, to build illegally by encroaching on to what remained of the common lands and building their crude 'Ty unos' *night house* type dwelling and thus giving birth to new communities.

In 1839 a survey was done of the fields and footpaths surrounding the farm of Hendre Fawr and some interesting old field names have thus been preserved. The fields adjacent to the footpath are: Cae Cyd (*common field*), Llain (*strip*) Llain randres (*shareland strip*) Two fields away from the footpath in the direction of Trefor lies Cae Llidiard Offeiriad (*field of the priest's hurdle*). This name may indicate that some land was granted to the township by the church. The field to the right of the wall, just before the wood, and through which the footpath passes is called Pant y Diogi (*hollow of laziness*).

The church lands here belonged to the ecclesiastical settlement under St Aelhaearn who was a follower of Beuno. This religious settlement is demonstrably ancient as three inscribed stones were discovered in 1865 in the vicinity of the church, one in a field called Gardd y Sant (*garden of the saint*) bears the inscription ALIORTVS ELMETIACO/HIC IACET 'Aliortus the Elmetian, he lies (here).' This commemorated the burial of a visitor, maybe a churchman, from the Celtic kingdom of Elmet in Yorkshire, north of Leeds.

# WALK 6: GARN FADRYN

—— ROAD

----- FOOTPATH

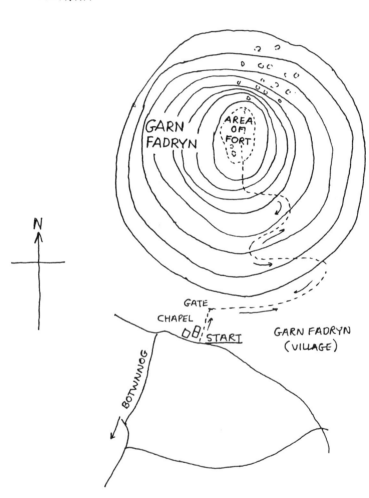

N

*Walk 6*

# Garn Fadryn

**½ an hour**

*Not too strenuous, and the views from the summit are some of the best on the peninsula.*

Park at the telephone box next to the chapel in the village, and follow the lane beside the chapel heading uphill until you reach a gate, enter this and turn right following the path around the hillside until after a short walk the path turns left and you begin your zig zag uphill walk to the summit.

**Notes on Garn Fadryn Fort**

This large hillfort with two pre-Roman phases of fortification and a later small summit fort, bears close parallel with Garn Boduan, described in a previous walk (No. 3). The period and circumstances of the fortifications have also been described in the notes on walk No. 3.

Phase 1 at Garn Fadryn c.300 B.C. covers an area of 12 acres enclosed by a stone wall. The second phase covers an area of 26 acres. This is a dissimilarity with Boduan in which the areas enclosed by the two phases of building differed only marginally. Exactly why the second phase at Fadryn was over double the area of the first is not known, although obviously, a local increase in population offers itself in explanation but this is by no means certain. As with Boduan, the round huts are probably to be associated mainly with the second phase c.100 B.C. It seems, though, that some huts classed as 'Tre'r Ceiri type' may be of later date and indicate occupation and building during the period of the Roman occupation. Due to the much slighter vegetation and greater preponderance of scree areas in which these huts are built, makes them much more discernible to the casual visitor than those on Boduan.

There are one or two interesting features on this site (see plan)

# PLAN OF HILLFORT ON GARN FADRYN

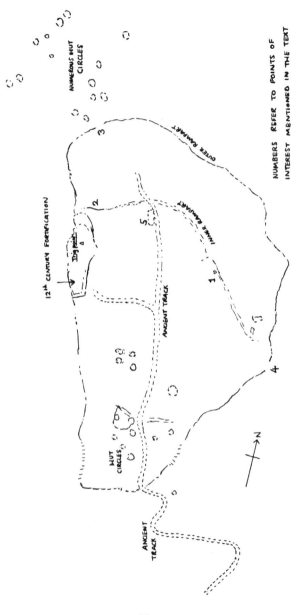

NUMBERS REFER TO POINTS OF
INTEREST MENTIONED IN THE TEXT

they are identified in these notes by their approximate true bearing and distance from the trigonometrical station on the summit.

1. A cist burial site (77 degrees 160 metres): A cist grave is one in which the burial is delineated by stone slabs set vertically forming a 'box' around the body. This cist originally measured around 2½ metres by 1½ metres. The east side is now ruined. Cists were usually present in the centre of stone cairns and were intended to receive the principal burial. There is a scatter of loose boulders adjacent to the cist and this would suggest the former presence of a cairn robbed to build the nearby rampart. The cairn and cist is Bronze Age in date and almost certainly pre dates the fort, their only association being the accident of location.

2. Well preserved section of walling (20 degrees 30 metres): This section of the ramparts visible north of the summit seem to suggest that the average thickness was around 3 metres plus, but to have varied between 3 and 4 metres.

3. North gateway (240 degrees 230 metres): Each phase of fortification seems to have had a north and south gateway, all are so ruined that no details are visible except in the north gateway of the second period in which a revetment lining on each side of the passage way can be seen.

4. The gap in the east side of the earlier rampart is a later break (95 degrees 230 metres) and may be comparatively modern.

5. A 'long building' close to the footpath (75 degrees 110 metres): This may be contemporary with the much later (12th century) summit fortification.

The latest defences on Garn Fadryn are, with marked similarity to Boduan, on the summit and occupy a small fraction of the area of the larger fort. To a large extent this stone-walled defensive system greatly utilises the existing rocky crag. The form of the ground shows some resemblance to the layout of a motte and bailey (for description of motte and bailey see section on Nefyn history), and although no mortar has been used in the stone work and there is little similarity to other mediaeval stone-work, there is little doubt

*Junction between phase (1) and phase (2) ramparts*

*View towards Yr Eifl from Garn Fadryn*

that this fortification represents the castle mentioned by Gerald of Wales in 1188. See note 2 walk No. 1. In his book 'The Journey through Wales' he begins chapter 6:

'We crossed the Traeth Mawr and the Traeth Bychan. These are two arms of the sea, one large and one small. Two stone castles have been built there recently. The one called Deudraeth belongs to the sons of Cynan and is situated in the Eifionydd area, facing the northern mountains. The second, which is called Carn Madryn, belongs to the sons of Owain: [Owain Gwynedd d.1170] it is on the Llŷn peninsula, on the other side of the river, and it faces the sea. 'Traeth' in the Welsh language means a tract of sand where the tide comes in, but which is left bare when the sea ebbs.'

# WALK 7: NEFYN — PORTHDINLLAEN

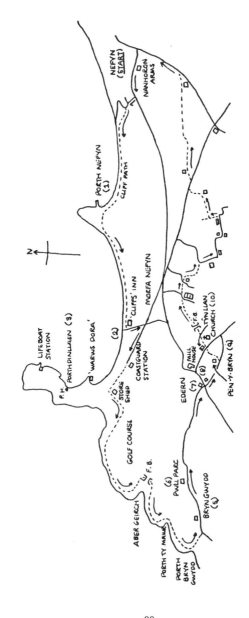

— — — ROAD

- - - - FOOTPATH

(1), (2), etc. NUMBERS FOR HISTORY NOTES

# Nefyn – Porth Dinllaen

3½ hours

*This walk begins as a cliff top walk with beautiful scenery, passing Porth Dinllaen, commonly regarded as one of the most picturesquely set villages on the Llŷn peninsula, boasting probably the prettiest and most atmospheric pub, set right on the beach. The return walk, although not bristling with historical and archaeological nuggets, is nevertheless through countryside seldom walked or seen. The road from Edern will take you back to town quicker, but our route is worth the extra mile or two.*

The walk begins from the centre of Nefyn at the roundabout, take the Aberdaron road and then turn right immediately after passing the garage and school on the left. This road is the way down to the beach *(traeth)*.

As you are approaching the beach take the footpath that runs alongside the 'castellated' house above the road. This path runs above the beach,[1] stay on it until you are approaching the end of the beach and then at a stone and earth wall *(clawdd)* turn left onto the tarmac road and then right, after about a 100 metres or so, turn right off the hard surface and onto a grass track which will take you onto the headland. At the fork, take the one on the left which will bypass the end of the headland and bring you back on to the cliff top path heading in the direction of Morfa Nefyn. Head along this ignoring all paths leading off it. Parts of the coastal path is dangerous – but signs mark out new routes to follow when necessary.

The village of Porth Dinllaen which runs along the beach and is complete with its own beautifully picturesque pub has now been bought by the National Trust. The beaches along this stretch of the coast, apart from being some of the best in the area are also some of the most underused.

At the paths-end on descending a long flight of steps,[2] turn left and head up the hill on the road away from the beach,

*View from cliff top path towards Yr Eifl*

*Village of Porth Dinllaen*

continuing until you reach the crossroads, here you will turn right and you will now be on the road to the golf club. Keep on this until you reach a gate which will take you onto the links, this gate is locked but there is a small pedestrian gate alongside. The path runs down to the right to the village and headland of Porth Dinllaen[3] and its lifeboat station, which is usually open to visitors and is well worth a visit. Return by same path to continue the walk.

A short way from the golf club gates you will come to a large building on your left, which is the groundsman's hut, turn left off the hard path and onto the grass. You will now be on the links themselves heading towards the gap in the trees on the skyline, after 100 metres or so a wall leads off to the left but you will bear right here at 45 degrees and head off towards the edge of the cliff.

Keep to this cliff edge until you come upon a small cove called Aber Geirch, cross the wooden stile here and head down into the small valley, cross the stream over the bridge and take the grass track up the other side of the valley. Enter the field gate and get back onto the cliff edge path, cross over the next picturesque bay, called Porth Tŷ Mawr[4] carrying along the cliff path until you come to the next beautiful cove called 'Porth Bryn Gwydd'.

Here you will leave the sea behind you and head inland, walk up through the valley and then onto a tarmac lane, turn left passing after a hundred metres or so a farm house called Bryn Gwydd,[5] and continue along this lane passing a driveway to another farm called Pwll Parc[6] and continue on to the main road.

This is Edern village and when you reach the crossroads, the house on your left on the corner called Heulwen is where another historian Eddie Kenrick[7] used to live, he produced a magazine about the area in the 40's and 50's.

Go straight over the crossroads passing the chapel in front of you[8] Continue up the road for about 200 metres and on the left you will come across a footpath sign pointing down a lane to a house called Pen y Bryn.[9] At the end of the drive turn right onto a path through the trees, cross the stone step stile and cross the field following the line of the telegraph poles. Continue on to the next stile leading to a lane and turn left, after some 30 metres turn right into a farm yard Ty'n Llan. Keep to this path, passing

Edern church[10]. After this go through a kissing gate and then a stream, keep to the hedge on your right, follow this path until it emerges onto a road, turn left here and after about 40 metres at the end of a garden with a white painted rockery, turn right into a wooded path. When the path emerges onto the road turn left and then immediately right at Pwll Crwn, follow the path through the kissing gate and head across a field onto a road again, turn right here.

Pass a cottage called Llain Fadryn. At the cottage called Buarth turn left onto a footpath going through a field gate, keep to the hedge on your right, after a short walk cross the hedge about midway down its length, cross over a stone step stile and head along the field boundary. Coming eventually to a stile, crossing this brings you out onto a lane, turn right and head along this lane until it emerges onto a main road. Turn right and walk for about 200 metres turning off the road onto a lane heading towards a cottage Tŷ Mawr. Pass the cottage and head through the kissing gate, keep straight on, with the hedge on your right, over the next stone step stile and follow the green lane, which, after a short walk emerges onto a tarmac lane. Cross over this and head immediately into a field, proceed in the direction of the hill in front of you Garn Boduan. Cross the wooden stile and turn right, go through the kissing gate and onto the main Nefyn-Pwllheli road, turn left onto this road and continue into the town.

## History Notes

[1] Throughout the centuries, Nefyn's history has always been infinitely bound up with the sea. As well as the ever present herring fishing industry. Nefyn was also famous for another maritime 'product'; seamen and sea captains. Very many families during the last century had all, or nearly all, of their male members at sea; either as ships' boys, able seamen, bosuns, masters or master mariners. The whole community was tuned to the tides, the seasons, the weather, and during storms, anxiety over loved ones at sea was an experience shared in almost every home in the village.

As well as the coastal trade there were ships and seamen involved in the trans-oceanic trade, with Australia, the Far East, North and South America, South Africa, indeed all over the world. Nefyn had a great many 'Cape Horners'. It has been said, that per head of population, Nefyn was the home of more master mariners than anywhere else in Britain. There were many families in which the tradition of seamanship spanned many generations. Such a family is commemorated on a tombstone in Nefyn church; the first recorded mariner in this family was Harry, son of Richard who was the son of William, born in 1690. His son David Parry is also recorded as a mariner and innkeeper at Y Plas, Nefyn. The tombstone is for his son Richard Davies and his family, it reads:

'Underneath are interred the remains of two infants of Richard Davies of this town, Mariner, by Elinor his wife; Robert who died 13th March, 1803 aged 8 months and Ann who died 3rd April, 1807 aged 9 months. Also in memory of Elinor, the first wife of the said Richard Davies who was interred 12th March, 1811 aged 34 years. Also the above named Richard Davies, who departed this life 1st of January, 1839 aged 70 years. Also Anne the daughter of Richard Davies by Elinor his wife who died 26th April, 1841 aged 31 years. Also his daughter Jane, wife of Captain Seth Williams who died 20th June, 1858 aged 58 years.'

Many of the large Victorian houses in Nefyn were built by master mariners who had made good livings in their overseas trade. Some made better livings than others, it depended on how much a share of the ship was owned by the master, it was usual for a ship to be owned by a company, or, as was mostly the case in this area, by a number of local entrepreneurial individuals. The 'shares' in a ship were always divided into '64ths', very rarely did one person own all 64 shares, sometimes the master would own the majority of the shares and thus gain the lions share of the profit, from the trading of that particular ship.

The ships plying in-and-out of the main ports of this area, Porth Dinllaen, Nefyn, Pwllheli, showed the full range of sailing ship types, ranging from small coastal smacks and schooners through the larger schooners of two or three masts, brigs, brigantines, barques and barquentines, to the majestic fully-rigged ships. The schooner was distinctive in having a large fore-and-aft mainsail on the fore mast and also on the main mast. The 'topgallant' schooner had one or two square-rigged topgallant sails braced on yards above the fore-and-aft main sail. The brig was a two masted vessel square-rigged on both masts. The schooner rig gradually ousted that of the brig in popularity. The brigantine was a cross between the two types of rigging, it was square rigged on the fore mast and for-and-aft on the main mast. The barque was a three masted craft, square rigged on the fore mast and main mast and fore and aft rigged on the jigger mast. The barquentine was also three-masted but was square-rigged only on the fore mast, the main and jigger masts being fore-and-aft. The 'ship' was a three or more masted vessel, square rigged on each mast. This was described as a 'full-rigger'.

Many of these beautiful sailing vessels were built locally. Pwllheli and Nefyn being the main ship building ports on Llŷn. The late 18th century saw the commencement of large-scale ship building at Nefyn — as opposed to the construction of small fishing boats and coastal smacks which had taken place for centuries. By the nineteenth century it was a major industry, and between 1810 and 1880, 191 ships were built on Nefyn beach in the area in front of the cottages. Probably the most famous of the shipbuilders at Nefyn was John John Thomas, known as 'Brennen Nefyn'. Between 1813 and 1840 he had constructed 30 vessels and is reported to have given employment to 300 carpenters. Here is a list of some of the Nefyn-built sailing ships:

*Waterloo*
> Bg (Brig) 104tn (tons) 69.7 (ft long)/18.5 (beam)/10.8 (depth of hold).
> Built 1815
> Capsized and sunk in collision with a whale, 50 miles north of Lowestoft on 21st March, 1855.
> All crew were saved and taken to Calais.

*Thetis*

Sr (schooner) 62tn, 52.6/17.5/10.3.
Built 1830.
R. Jones, master.

*John & Mary*

Sr. Built by John Thomas in 1831, lost 1841.
Known locally as 'Bwgan Llŷn' (The Ghost of Llŷn).

*Three Brothers*

Sr. 92tn, 64.8/21.3/10.8.
Built 1845.
Owner J. Roberts, W. Jones master.

*Herbert*

Sr, 76tn, 67.1/18.6/10.6.
Built in 1848. Condemned in 1899.
John Thomas, Borth-y-gest, master.
Later owned by D. Morris & Co., Porthmadog.

*Zedulous*

Sr, 76tn.
Built 1849 by R. Thomas. Was lost on Porthmadog Bar in
1882 carrying a cargo of copper ore and dynamite.

*Mary Watkins*

Sr, 169tn. 91.0/23.3/12.7.
Built 1850. Lost 1888.
Captain Watkins, Cricieth master.

*Linus*

Bkn (Barquentine) formerly a Bg.
189tn. 105.6/22.7/13.5.
Built 1857.
With her Captain Evan Henry Williams in command this
ship was regarded as the fastest in the area, comparable with a

clippership. A story is told to illustrate her speed; a group of thirteen ships were making for Gibraltar, the *Linus* appeared on the horizon behind them one morning, sailed straight through the group and by dusk was out of sight ahead of them.

### Maria Jane

Sr, 99tn. 78.2/21.2/10.7.
Built 1857.
G. Williams of Porthmadog owned 64/64ths.

### Ann Jane

Sr. 109tn. 76.7/21.5/11.5.
Built 1858.
Was owned by a Barmouth business man Robert Jones.
Lost off the coast of Anglesey on a voyage from London to Caernarfon in 1898 carrying a cargo of 175 tons of cement.

### Ellen

Sr. 140tn.
Built 1858.
Lost on Grassholm Island on the Pembrokeshire coast. All hands were saved except Captain Thomas Davies who was later found dead on the wreck having been eaten by rats.

### Nanhoron

Bn (Brigantine). 147tn. 92.6/22.7/12.2.
Built 1858.
Owned outright by her Captain, Hugh Williams.
Lost near the mouth of the Elbe in January 1899 on a voyage from Hamburg to Londonderry with a cargo of 233 tons of salt.

### Jane & Ann

Sr. 74tn. 66.5/20.2/10.5.
Built 1860 by Robert Thomas and was owned by Griffith and

Co., Bangor.

*Jane Hughes*
Built 1861 and owned outright by R. Owens.

*Glanavon*
Bg. 184tn. 96.0/21.0/13.0.
Built 1862 by Owen Griffith.
First owned by John Timothy of Borth-y-gest later by Jarret
& Co. for the South American trade.
Lost on Christmas Day 1884.

*Polly Preston*
Sr. 131tn. 89.6/22.6/11.7.
Built 1863 by Robert Thomas.
David Nicholas captain.
Lost with all hands on a voyage from Bremerhaven to
Scotland on 2nd September, 1903.

*Miss Thomas*
Sr. 127tn. 80/21.5/11.8.
Built 1864 by Robert Thomas.
Traded in the Baltic, Elbe and Morocco.
Had to be re-keeled in Landskrona, Sweden after being
driven ashore in a storm.

*John Davies*
Sr. 89tn. 71/20/10.
Built 1867.
Owned by Davies & Co. Caernarfon
Lost off Cork.

*Joseph Nicholson*
Sr. 99tn.
Built 1868 by Robert Thomas.
The ship was lost in collision with another Nefyn ship the

*Walter Ulric* which survived. The collision occurred off St Tudwal's Islands, Abersoch.

*Planet*
> Sr. 138tn.
> Built 1872.
> Later renamed *Minna Elkan*.
> Lost on the river Elbe 15th Decenmber, 1899.

*Clara Felicia*
> Sr. Later rigged as a ketch.
> 89tn. 75/21/11.2.
> Built 1874. Sold in Bridgewater 1896.

*Walter Ulric*
> Sr. 98tn. 85.8/22.5/10.9.
> Built 1875.
> She was a Baltic and Morocco trader and was sunk by enemy action in the First World War off Land's End, after having survived a collision with *Joseph Nicholson* off Abersoch.
> The ownership details of this ship are a good example of how fragmented and complex such ownership could be, at one time she was owned by:
>
> Richard Hughes, Porthmadog 20/64ths
> Rees Evans, Porthmadog slate agent 16/64ths
> Robert Roberts, Porthmadog, clerk, 16/64ths
> John Farmer Sims, Porthmadog, quarry manager, 4/64ths
> William Evans, Junior, Porthmadog, grazier, 4/64ths
> Charles Nicholson, Newcastle on Tyne, slate merchant 4/64ths.
>
> In February 1894 all 64 shares were bought by Evan Williams, of Porthmadog who then sold the ship to Cornish Traders Ltd., in 1916. The vessel was lost in 1917.

*Annie Lloyd*
> Bn. 149tn. 95.5/23.5/12.4.

Built 1876, lost on Fortune Island in the West Indies on March 6th, 1907.

*Ellen Lloyd*

Bg. 182tn. 100.5/24.6/13.2.

Built in 1877 by Griffith Owen and at first named *Ebenezer Parry* and was sold at Fowey in 1912 as the *Robert Marguerite*. Her captain (as the Ellen Lloyd) was Evan Morris. A fascinating story is told of this man by Emrys Hughes and Aled Eames in their famous book 'Porthmadog Ships' (from which the details of these Nefyn ships are taken, and is a masterly book which should be consulted by anyone seriously interested in the maritime history of North Wales). When sailing off Newfoundland Captain Morris was washed overboard, but by dint of being a powerful swimmer he was able to get back on board. The crew were convinced that the ship was lost and had taken to the rigging, the ship was out of control with the wheel spinning freely. Captain Morris ran to the wheel which knocked him down breaking his leg in three places, he removed some broken splinters of bone from his leg with a pair of scissors and managed to hang on to the wheel and regain control of the ship. Other run-of-the-mill maritime disasters experienced by Captain Morris included the sinking of the *Menai Straits* which caught fire when rounding the Horn, Morris subsequently spent 19 days in an open boat before ultimately landing in the Falkland Islands. He experienced a mutiny while in command of the *Sarmation*, a rull-rigger carrying 'Coolies' from Calcutta to Demerara. He quelled the uprising by shooting the ring leader.

*Venus*

Sr. 83/22.1/11.5.

Built in 1880 by Griffith Owen.

This ship has achieved immortality as being the last ship to be built at Nefyn.

To round off this section, here is a list of a few events connected with the maritime story of Nefyn arranged in a chronological order.

1287 — In this year 63 people from Nefyn owned nets and a few boats.

1726 — There are smuggling riots in Nefyn.

1729 — A customs officer is appointed for the port.

1748 — In this year 5,000 casks of herrings were sold in Nefyn.

1760 — The first ship built in Nefyn, the *Hopewell*.

1762 — 'Fleet of ships' carried herrings from Nefyn to Cork and Dublin.

1796 — French capture the Nefyn sloop *Felicity*.

1843 — 'Pwllheli & Nefyn Mutual Marine Insurance Co.' was formed.

1845 — The sloop *Pilot* was wrecked at Nefyn and also in the same year the Pwllheli built ship *Elizabeth Grainge*.

1857 — A small schooner of Nefyn, the *Thomas* was lost off Holyhead.

1866 — The formation in Nefyn of the 'Provincial Shipowners Marine Protection Society' and the 'Provincial A.1 Mutual Marine Insurance Co'.

1868 — Sees the formation of the 'The Ancient Briton Mutual Marine Insurance Society' followed by, in:

1869 — 'The Cambrian Freight & Outfit Insurance Co'.

1872 — The formation of two more insurance companies namely the 'Victoria Mutual Marine Insurance Society' and the 'North Wales Mutual Marine Insurance Co.' both based in Nefyn.

1877 — In this year another company was set up in Nefyn, not an insurance company this time, it was the 'Ancient Briton Iron Sailing Ship Co'.

1878 — The various insurance companies then in existence in Nefyn valued all their ships collectively in excess of two million pounds.

1879 — A steam ship, the *SS Baron* was in danger in a storm in

Nefyn bay, all the crew were saved.
In the same year the 'North and South Wales Iron Sailing Ship Freight & Outfit Co' was formed in Nefyn.

And a last gasp for the marine insurance companies in Nefyn:

1881    — Saw the formation of the 'The Caernarfon & Nefyn Mutual Marine Insurance Co', and the 'Caernarfon and Nefyn shipowners Mutual Marine Protection Association Co'.
1884    — The 'Prydain Steam Ship Co.' set up in Nefyn.
1890    — The 'Pwllheli and Nefyn Mutual Marine Insurance Co.' formed in 1843 is wound up.

This tongue twisting list of marine insurance companies and the various shipping and chandlery companies coming into existence in the latter half of the nineteenth century, is a testament to the vigorous life of the world of ships and the sea which was the heart and soul, in those years, of the little town of Nefyn.

For anyone interested in the Maritime history of Nefyn, a visit to the maritime museum in St Mary's church (opened in 1979) is essential. It has many interesting exhibits, and under the helmsmanship of Mr Gwilym Evans, a retired schoolmaster from Morfa Nefyn, the number of exhibits is increasing year-by-year along with the reputation of the museum.

[2] There was a brickworks on top of the cliff just across the road at this point, its tall chimney was a prominent landmark. The brickworks was in production between 1868 and 1906. From 1893 to 1899 two Edern business men were in partnership running the works.

Interestingly we have some information as to when Morfa Nefyn beach began to attract tourists. Ref. John Hughs states in his memoirs that these first visitors appeared in the area around 1870.

Early in this century there were two other pubs on the beach at Porthdinllaen in addition to the Tŷ Coch, there were the Whitehall and the Tŷ Gwyn.

[3] Porthdinllaen, surely one of the most picturesque natural harbours' in Wales. The Reverend Bingley in his book 'North Wales and its Scenery' (1798) describes it thus after having passed through Nefyn:

'Descending from hence to the shore, the traveller will arrive at Porthdinelbyn [sic], *the Harbour in Llŷn*, about a mile distant. Here are a few houses situated at the foot of a small semicircular range of low mountains, with, in front, a large and extensive bay. The place is even more secluded from the world than Nevin; it cannot be seen except from the edges of the hills that immediately surround it. The entire extent of land betwixt the hills and the sea is so small, as scarcely to be more than a mile and a half across, and a quarter of a mile deep. The harbour is chiefly frequented by coasting and Irish vessels.'

As for the name Porthdinllaen, we have seen it rendered as 'The Harbour in Llŷn', it has also appeared as 'Porth-dinlleyn' with a translation 'haven of the low-lying fortress'. To our minds, however, a commentator one 'J.R.' adding a footnote to Thomas Pennant's use of the names 'Dinthlayn' and 'Porth yn Llŷn' comes much nearer the mark;

'*Dinthlayn* means of course *Dinllayn*, which is now pronounced *Din Llaen*, and I suspect that Pennant's *Porth yn Llŷn* has been slightly mended from *Porthdin Llaen*, since it is now always called either *Porth Din Llaen* or Port Dinllaen. There would thus seem to have been two words, Lleyn *lagin-i* and *Llaen, lagin-a;* we have a cognate word in *Leinster*, which, stripped of its Scandinavian ending, was in old Irish, *Lagin*, from *Lagin* a spear.'

He goes on to make an interesting little aside:

'The map-makers who insist on writing *Llaen* as *Llyen*, because the Port is in Lleyn, are not likely to allow the natives a voice in the matter.'

This sounds about 'par for the course!'

Most of the history of Porthdinllaen is, like that of Nefyn, closely tied to the sea, and as in the section on Nefyn, it may be of interest to present some of this history in a short chronological list:

1587 — A French privateer is grounded at Porthdinllaen.

1716 — Customs build a store house at Porthdinllaen.

1763 — Smuggling cutter unloaded a cargo of rum.

1767 — Sloop *Nancy* built in Edern (Porthdinllaen?)

1785 — Customs officials strike back by arresting the crew of a smuggling cutter caught on rocks in Porthdinllaen bay. But the upper hand returns to the smugglers for in —

1791 — A smuggling lugger outruns a customs boat and escapes.

1804 — In this year 656 ships use Porthdinllaen.

1807 — This year saw the commencement of the building of piers in Porthdinllaen, and also of a pub the 'Whitehall'.

1808 — The formation of the Porthdinllaen Harbour Co. with the princely sum of 12,000 pounds at its disposal.

1815 — Further building of piers and landing platforms.

1817 — Ship wrecked in Porthdinllaen with total loss of life.

1825 — 612 ships loaded cargo at Porthdinllaen.

1843 — A steamship *SS Monk* en route from Porthdinllaen to Liverpool with a cargo of pigs was wrecked on Caernarfon sand bar, 20 people were drowned.
In the same year many ships were grounded at Porthdinllaen in heavy storms. 900 ships use Porthdinllaen.

1846 — A brig from Glasgow wrecked in the bay with the loss of all hands.

1852 — The schooner *Silah* is wrecked at Porthdinllaen.

1859 — Two ships lost this year the *Laura Ellen* and the *Princess Charlotte*.

1861 — 715 ships use Porthdinllaen.

1863 — Schooner *Bardsey* wrecked in Porthdinllaen. On December 3rd Robert Rees of Morfa Nefyn won the R.N.L.I. bronze medal for saving 23 lives from the ship *Bodfel* and 'numerous others' on that stormy day.

1864 — A lifeboat station was built at Porthdinllaen to house the first lifeboat the *Cotton Shepperd* which soon had its work cut out as in one day in this year 13 ships were wrecked.

1866 — Loss of brigantine *Columbia*.
1867 — Schooner *Six Brothers* wrecked in the bay.
1870 — Another schooner the *Nymph* lost at Porthdinllaen.
1873 — A brief respite from the list of lost ships; the brig *Sybile Wynne* launched at Porthdinllaen.
1877 — *Rebecca and May* lost at Porthdinllaen, followed by the loss in
1878 — of the ship 'Velocity'.
1881 — Schooner *Miss Beck* sank in the bay.
1883 — *Lady Hinks* founders on rocks.
1886 — *Llysfaen* sinks at Porthdinllaen.
1888 — The name-sake of the lifeboat *George Moore* founders on rocks on the tip of the headland.
1894 — A fishing smack from Jersey the *Dauntless* is wrecked in Porthdinllaen.
1910 — Into the 20th century and the catalogue of shipwrecks continues, this year the ketch *Sarah*
1926 — A new slipway is constructed to accommodate the new lifeboat at Porthdinllaen. This was the first motor lifeboat service on Llŷn.
1927 — A steamship the *SS Matje* runs aground on the beach.
1930 — The coastguard station is founded at Porthdinllaen.
1933 — Three R.A.F. flying boats crashed at Porthdinllaen. They were pulled ashore and re-floated.
1934 — The only female harbour master in Wales, Mrs Jones of the Tŷ Coch Inn, Porthdinllaen died this year.
1940 — A Dutch ship is towed to Porthdinllaen after having been bombed and fired off Bardsey.

The large building raised above the sand on the Southwest end of Morfa Nefyn beach, just before Porthdinllaen bay looks like a warehouse, this is in fact what it is. It is known as 'Warws Dora' (Dora's warehouse). The Aberdovey and Barmouth Steamship Company, owned a few small steamships mostly employed in the coastal trade between Liverpool, Porthdinllaen, Aberdovey and

Barmouth carrying cargos of groceries and general provisions, including timber carried on deck. The steamship *Dora*, one of their vessels was a much loved and familiar sight at Porthdinllaen and around the Welsh coast.

The warehouse was built to service these steamships, especially the *Dora*. This ship was built in 1900 by J. Fullerton & Co., at Paisley and was a 296 ton steel screw vessel. A well known sea captain from Morfa Nefyn David Williams became Captain of the *Dora* in 1909. Not only was the ship indispensable to traders and builders of Llŷn she also provided a useful means of passenger travel to Liverpool, and many local people would avail themselves for a shopping trip to the city, returning with their purchases stacked up on the deck.

Captain Williams was a vastly experienced mariner serving twice in sailing vessels before steam vessels, and although his long command of the *Dora* was mostly trouble free, even he had some sticky moments. One such occasion, brought about by the sudden oneset of thick fog as the *Dora* was approaching Porthdinllaen, caused Captain Williams some concern. He decided that it would be dangerous to come into the port in such thick fog, so instead, he would anchor up in the bay and wait for visibility to return, manoeuvring the ship into a seemingly safe position in which to drop anchor. It was not until the following dawn that the fog lifted, and when it did it was seen that the *Dora* was anchored, not in the safety of Porthdinllaen bay, but on the other side of the headland at Borthwen and perilously close to some rocks! a narrow escape indeed.

The sad final moments of the *Dora* were witnessed by Captain Williams. The ship had been commandeered in 1914 to aid in the war effort and was set to trade between Liverpool and Belfast. On the 1st May, 1917 returning from Belfast in ballast she was intercepted by a German submarine just off the coast of Galloway. Captain Williams was ordered by the German commander to abandon ship and take to the lifeboats. When this was done the *Dora* was torpedoed. David Williams and his crew eventually came ashore at Galloway.

The whole of Llŷn in the nineteenth century, not just the villages on the coast, was permeated with the tang of the sea. Many farms had paintwork done with the noticeable care which was applied to the painting of the ships. (Old black-and-white photographs obviously do not convey the fact that these ships were often brightly coloured.) Many houses had old sea chests for storage, and the painting of a sailing ship hanging in the parlour was almost obligatory. Dotted around many farmhouses, on mantelpiece, shelf, sideboard or Welsh dresser could be seen many small ornaments and momentos from around the world.

Porthdinllaen today presents us with a picturesque and idyllic face, but its fate almost became vastly different. It was thought that Porthdinllaen could be developed as a harbour to rival Holyhead and become the main port for traffic with Ireland. As early as 1770 proposals had been made:

'. . . . for making a turnpike road from Llangynog in Montgomeryshire though Bala to Traeth Mawr, for embanking and draining the sands of Traeth Mawr and for continuing the said road to Porth-dyn-llaen in the bay of Caernarvon, in addition to the advantages of Agriculture, the design would open a shorter and readier road from London to Dublin than any in use at present, shorter than the Holyhead road through Chester by thirty-seven miles. If the packed-boats were landed at Porth-dyn-llaen, and this were made the General Post Road the conveying of Mail would gain time in proportion; it would be the road for travellers and it would bring much wealth to the country.'

The decision for these proposals rested with the government, but the first of them, the construction of the road, went ahead in anticipation of a favourable governmental response. When, by the narrowest of margins, the development of the harbour at Porthdinllaen was rejected, there was tremendous disappointment. Much other preliminary work had been done; a landing place for ships had been designed, an extensive survey of the harbour had been commissioned, and plans had been drawn up for the building of a large hotel. Many people had put a great deal of money into the scheme, notable among them was William Alexander

Madocks (who was later to be responsible for much land reclamation and the building of 'the cob' in Porthmadog).

The Porthdinllaen Turnpike Trust Act was passed on May 17th, 1803. The road started in Porthdinllaen and went inland for about three miles where it forked, one line going straight across towards Cricieth, the other via Boduan to Pwllheli, the roads were re-united near Llanystumdwy. The route then continued from Cricieth through Tremadog, Beddgelert and Nant Gwynant to Capel Curig.

Apart from Trustees and subscribers like William Madocks the income of the Trust was to be had from charging tolls for the users of the road and for this purpose toll-gates were erected. Although the rejection by Parliament of the Porthdinllaen harbour development scheme dealt a mortal blow to the fortunes of the turnpike road the Porthdinllaen Turnpike Trust limped along, under perpetual financial difficulties for a total of sixty one years. The Trust was to 'continue in being until November 1st, 1874 and no longer', it expired on that day. The provision of funds for the maintenance of the road was a major problem right from the outset. Edmund Hyde-Hall in about 1810 describing Porthdinllaen harbour:

'In the little road, which is of fine sand surrounded by some high ground and protected, as has been observed, by the headland to the north-west, nature has provided a recess from Caernarfon Bay so nearly land-locked as to be only open to the north-east. Hither small vessels had from time to time run for shelter, and here also was an establishment upon a small scale of boats engaged in the herring fishery. In the progressive intercourse between Great Britain and Ireland this port has been pitched upon as the point of departure and arrival, which might prove convenient to the public and not unprofitable to the undertaker.'

Elsewhere he says:

'To this harbour a turnpike road has been brought with the view of establishing along this line a communication with Ireland. Towards doing this no great progress certainly had been made when I visited the place. The road was unworn by a wheel, and was in fact hastening to bury itself without disturbance beneath a coating of herbage.'

He goes on to say:

' . . . the protection afforded by the headland had been already extended by the erection of a small pier, and of it many small vessels had habitually awaited themselves, and no less than twenty six such vessels at the time of my visiting it were riding behind it. But this accommodation was very scanty in proportion to what was required. It required therefore either to be enlarged or replaced upon a much more extensive scale; pacquetes were to be built or bought, captains' houses erected, hotels formed, tenanted and furnished; and above all a town established in the place of the half dozen small houses already raised.'

'The inconveniences and, in truth, the dangers of the passage from Ireland to Liverpool . . . were too well known; while the incivility and impositions practised at Holyhead were such as to make every traveller desirous of seeing a competition at least brought about by giving him a choice of routes. Public expectation was studiously set afloat throughout the county and along the roads, and the conversation of the county for a while turned very commonly upon the topic. Improvements were talked of, and the number of persons employed mentioned; so that I directed my course to the place eager to see what had been already done, and full of anticipation with respect to the remaining advantages. There were half a dozen carpenters at work laying down the flooring of an inn, what was to be the new pier was already a sort of ruin, and the beneficial effects of the old one were said to have been materially abridged. Holyhead is in no danger of an immediate rivalship.'

And so the picturesque tranquility and remoteness of Porthdinllaen is preserved. Too often though, places like this are seen only from the point of view of the tourist. If the proposed developments had taken place it would have brought much needed jobs and prosperity to the area, then and now. The whole of the Llŷn peninsula would have assumed a much different quality and the picture postcard vista, of Porthdinllaen at least, would have gone forever, but uppermost in many people's minds, past, and present, is the desperate need for local jobs. An ideal situation of course, but one very difficult to achieve, is a balance between the preservation of the unique countryside of Llŷn and sensitive development to provide work. The hamlet of Porthdinllaen has very recently been purchased by the National Trust and so its preservation is ensured, but let's hope this preservation is not of the 'glass case' variety.

4 Porth Tŷ Mawr and Cwmistir (the next bay along) are the scenes of three locally famous shipwrecks. Just after the turn of the century the *SS Stuart* went ashore at Tŷ Mawr in a gale. The ship was carrying a wide range of goods and the local people had a bit of a bonanza. Carpets, furniture, pots and pans were washed ashore along with food stuffs, and, best of all, whisky by the caseload. The whisky was spirited away in short measure to be hidden from any customs investigation and the hiding places used were ingenious, lofts, gardens, wells, haystacks, rabbit holes etc. The tradition goes that half the neighbourhood was drunk for many days to come!

*Porth Tŷ Mawr*

An old tradition still extant in Llŷn during the last century predicted that one day Llŷn would be invaded by the Irish, and many locals believed it. Quite where or when this tradition started is not known. It is certainly true that the Irish had once invaded this area but that was nearly two millennia in the past! In 1870, during the Franco-German war, a sailing ship the *Sorrento* came ashore at Tŷ Mawr and was wrecked. The sailors, who were American, managed to swim ashore and struggle up the cliffs to the old farmhouse at Tŷ Mawr and knocked on the door for assistance. Silence knelled inside the house until:

'Cadi, they've come at last,' shouted the old grandmother to her daughter.

'Who have?' she replied.

'Why the Irish, of course,' answered the old woman.

The man of the house, lit a rushlight, and taking down a musket from over the fire place cautiously approached the door. When he unlatched it he was bowled over by a rush of sodden sailors babbling at him in English which he did not understand, he babbled back in Welsh and they got nowhere. The captain still had his wits about him, and, even more miraculously a box of matches which he withdrew from his pocket. He laid the box on the table, removed three matches and stuck them in the box to represent the masts of a ship. Understanding dawned followed by a drying session around the fire accompanied by the drinking of whiskey produced from that praiseworthy pocket of the captain.

In 1881 another ship was wrecked, this time close by at Cwmistir. The ship was the *Cyprian* and foundered on the rocks on a wild stormy night. Harrowing cries of the sailors were heard throughout the night, the local people lit lanterns and stood on the cliff tops but were powerless to offer any assistance, the sea was much too rough. Most of the crew were drowned but a few managed to reach shore safely and were cared for by an old farmer. During the next day all sorts of wreckage started to come ashore, silks, china, clothes, and liquor and much more besides. Not wishing to look a gift horse in the mouth the locals distributed this ocean-borne largesse between themselves before customs officials came snooping around.

One old man, determined to outwit the customs officers went to the churchyard at night, removed the lid of a grave and stashed some fine silks within. After months had passed and the threatened visit by the customs had not materialised, he went back to the grave to recover his treasures only to find that they had completely rotted away.

5 There was an old lady of Edern, Margaret Dafydd, who was known to be one hundred years old in 1865. The farm on the left of the road just inland from Porth Bryngwydd, and called Bryngwydd, is believed to be where she lived.

6 The house called *Pwll Parc* is the home of a well known Edern sea-faring family. Captain John Williams was master of the full-rigged ship *Amoor* in 1875, as well as being the ships' master he was also her owner. Two of John Williams' sons Owen and Captain Watkin Williams became famous ship-owners by the turn of the century with their Cardiff based company 'Owen and Watkin Williams & Co'. He served on ten different company ships. His first command was in 1903 on the *SS Venedotian*, later in his career he was captain of the company's largest ship the *Silurian*. Another Edern mariner captain William Griffith, sailed on nine different vessels of the Owen and Watkin Williams Company. Captain Hugh Roberts, another Edern seaman, joined the company in 1908 after beginning his sea-faring career with the Newcastle Company.

A shipping company 'Hugh Roberts & Co. Newcastle' was established by a partnership between Edward Beck of Newcastle-on-Tyne and Hugh Roberts who was born in Edern in 1826. He married Ellen, daughter of Thomas Roberts of Bryngwydd Farm (mentioned above). Several of the earlier ships belonging to this company had 'Beck' in their names. Three of these ships were built in Porthdinllaen; the *Miss Beck*, *Fanny Beck* and *Edward Beck*. When the company later ventured into steamships he still retained, as crew, many seamen from Edern.

7 The house set back on the corner of the cross roads called Heulwen is where Eddie Kenrick used to live (see notes on Edern

village).

[8] The present chapel is on the same site as a former chapel that was built in 1842 and enlarged in 1877. The present building was erected in 1888.

[9] Pen-y-bryn is reputed to be one of the oldest if not the oldest house in the Edern area. It bears a date plaque of 1790 over the door but it was certainly built before then. It is known, for instance, that the kitchen was used as a chapel for many years before the first chapel was built in Edern in about 1775.

*Pen-y-bryn*

Mary Wiliams who inherited Pen-y-bryn married the Reverend John Jones when he came to this area from Anglesey in around 1787. John Jones became well known as John Jones, Edern. He was a highly respected minister locally and also over the whole of Llŷn. He worked tirelessly as a minster for 38 years and did monumental work in promoting methodism in Llŷn. He died in 1822.

[10] The church dedication of Edern may refer to Edeyrn or Eternus a son of Cunedda Wledig (see introduction).

The church was rebuilt on this site in 1867-8 using the footings of the original church of mediaeval date, at the same time a south transeptal chapel was added to give the church a cruciform plan. Some of the roof trusses were re-used from the old roof, two are to be found in the north chapel and date from the 15th century, and are of the arch-braced collar type. Another mediaeval roof truss has been used in the south chapel and is of plain type.

In the north chapel a chest can be seen constructed by the hollowing out of a log. This is also of mediaeval date.

In the early 19th century the east window was described as having 'some poor fragments of painted glass, as there are also in the windows of the north aisle.' Yet in around 1940 'A beautiful stained glass east window commemorates the death of Ref J.P. Jones-Parry, M.A. of Christchurch Oxon, who died in 1865' is described.

Members of the Griffith family of Cefnamlwch have, for generations have been buried at this church. There is a brass tablet on the wall in memory of the following family members:

> William Griffith of Llŷn died in 1688.
> Elizabeth, his wife, daughter of A. Calvely, Chester died in 1705.
> Hon. Elizabeth Griffith, widow of John Griffith and daughter of Viscount Williams Bukleley of Baron Hill, died 1715.
> William Griffith, died 1714.
> John Griffith, died 1739.
> William Griffith, died 1752.

William Griffith, who died in 1714 was 28 years old, John Griffith was 32 and William Griffith was 31 years of age. These early deaths of the male line of the family caused some problems. Hyde-Hall had an explanation:

'The premature deaths of so many males, and the final descent of the properties on females cannot but be remarked, and has been thus accounted for not only in this instance, but in the many others of which notice has already been taken. The women were sober; the men drank themselves to death. For this habit some apology may perhaps be found in remoteness of situation and rusticity of manners. Literature and refinement afforded neither object of pursuit nor topic of conversation, and the good fellowship of the evening was thus left to gratify itself as it could with a recapitulation of the morning's sports. The present resident gentry, secure of a very different character, may easily endure to have their forefathers thus spoken of.'

The large ash trees growing near the church and around the vicarage were planted in 1751 by the Rev. Andrew Edwards, then rector.

There is an unmarked grave in the churchyard where are buried the 19 victims of the *Cyprian* ship wreck in 1881 (see note 4). There is another grave bearing the skull-and-crossbones and another with only 'Here lieth' engraved upon it.

There is a local tradition that there was an earlier church nearer to the river and when a mill leat was dug in c.1850 some burials were found. There are no surface features at this spot (SH 28003975). Along with the burials an inscribed stone is also said to have been found.

# Edern

' . . . Some few trees are sprinkled about the church, but the parish is otherwise bare of trees, and is in general flat. Its agriculture maybe classed with that of Nefyn, with the concession perhaps of a somewhat better style of management. The chief proprietor within the parish is the Honourable Mrs Fynch, and in it lies one small common. A pretty translucent stream of no great force or volume runs through the village, and after turning a good sized corn mill below it, falls into the sea behind the headland by which the harbour of Porthdinllaen is formed.'

So was the parish and village described nearly two hundred years ago. The lower part of the village near the pub still retains much of its character from former years.

Edern was formerly the site of one of the main postal sorting offices for Llŷn, the other was at Sarn. The postal service was by a horse-drawn mail car and was started at Edern by Thomas Jones of the Ship Inn, sometime around the 1840's and was to remain in the hands of the Jones' family for over 100 years. Thomas Jones' son John carried on the work. He was a bard, musician and choirmaster, his bardic name was 'Edeyrnfab' (son of Edern).

Next in line was John Samuel Jones, also landlord of the Ship Inn. He was the only remaining private mail contractor when he retired in 1963. Another member of the Jones family, the Rev. Samuel Thomas Jones was born in 1852 and was to become an emminent Welsh preacher before his death in the Great War.

The mail route in those days, before trains came to Pwllheli, was by the four-in-hand Mail Coach from Caernarfon to Pwllheli, with a change of horses at St Beuno's Hotel at Clynnog Fawr, and then on to the Pwllheli Post Office. This Post Office stood in Penlan Street. An open gig was then used to convey the mail to the Llŷn sorting offices of Edern and then Sarn. Just outside Sarn, near Cefnamlwch was an old ramshackle hut called Beudy Begw (*Begw's Cowshed*). Begw was the village postwoman and she carried the letters to Llangwnnadl and beyond on foot. Letters destined for Rhiw and Aberdaron were also conveyed on foot from

Sarn.

This information is taken from one of Eddie Kenrick's guide books to the Llŷn peninsula. During the 30's and 40's Eddie was a newspaper reporter and it was in this time that he produced his guide books which he wrote, printed and published himself. Among the titles he produced were *Kenrick's Lleyn Peninsula*, *The Ancient Churches of Lleyn* and *Lleyn Sketches*. They are now local collectors items. From 1947 onwards, Eddie was postmaster at Edern for eighteen years. For part of his life he lived in the house on the corner of Y Groesffordd in Edern (mentioned in the last walk, note 7).

The *Ship Inn* (where, incidentally pigs were weighed weekly) was not the only pub in the village. Before the 1930's a second pub was situated a few doors further down the street towards the bridge called the *Cefnamlwch Arms*. Next door to the Ship Inn was a house connected with the old woollen mill and factory just across the road.

This factory was built in 1852 by John Williams of Ty'n Llan farm (situated just behind the site of the mill) just across the river from a flour mill. At that time a certain Robert William Rowlands, who was working in a similar factory in Sarn, heard of this new venture in Edern and came to see John Williams, whereupon, at the age of 20 he took over the tenancy of the new factory. (Robert William Rowlands had a son, Hugh Thomas Rowlands, and his son, Morris, was the father of Marjorie, wife of Nigel Burras, writing this now. It is Morris' wife and Marjorie's mother, Mary, who is to be thanked for this information on the woollen factory).

The first machinery, used in the factory was a locally made New Carding Machine. This was soon followed by a Spinning Jenny and a "Slubbing Billy", all worked by hand. The factory soon became established, producing a wide range of woollen goods. The ensuing increase in production put a strain on the working capacity of the original hand operated machinery and new water powered machinery was brought in to replace it. These machines proved to be a great boon to the production capacity of the factory. There was one drawback however; during the summer months if it was particularly dry there was often a lack of water in the river to drive the wheel. This situation was not too bad initially when the only water driven machine, in addition to the fulling mill, was a single combing machine, but when weaving, spinning and carding machines were introduced which all relied on water power, the seasonal lack of water became a major problem. The mill and factory provided a much needed source of employment for locals.

The house connected with the mill, next door to the Ship Inn was in fact a shop for the retail of the factory produce. It was run by Catherin Rowlands — wife of William Rowlands.

Goods produced by the factory and sold from the shop were distributed all over Llŷn. There is a surviving account book which lists 350 names of customers from such places as Llithfaen, Chwilog, Llaniestyn, Tudweiliog and Sarn. Some individual and enterprising methods of payment, when cash was short, are noted in the customers account book. For example:

1888 — account paid for by shoe repairs

1897 — received a 27½ lb pot of butter and in the same year a Christmas goose was presented in lieu of cash payment.

Mention has already been made in the history notes for the last walk (Note No. 6) on some of Edern's well known sea captains, mariners and ship owners, some others include:

Captain William Williams, Tirbedw, Edern
He was a member of a family packed with sea-farers. His father was a sea captain as were his three brothers, he was born in 1863. He married the daughter of Hugh Roberts' sister (Hugh Roberts was the founder of the Hugh Roberts & Co., shipping firm of Newcastle-on-Tyne, mentioned earlier). He sailed with the company until his death at an early age in 1903. His son William Williams of Morfa Nefyn was also a sea captain.

Captain William Williams, Rhianfa, Edern
He also sailed with the Newcastle Company and had family connections with Hugh Roberts' wife. He died in the Bay of Biscay in December 1893 when the ship *North Durham* on which he was master went missing.

Captain Thomas Williams, Angorfa, Edern

He was born in 1847 and went to sea at a very early age, and served as a cook on the *Miss Beck* on his second voyage earning 10/- (50p) a month. His first captaincy was of the *Fanny Beck* in 1870 which was lost at sea in 1880. He served most of his career with the Robert Hughes company. He died in 1933. (Angorfa is the large house on the left hand side of the main road on the crest of the hill as you leave Edern on the Tudweiliog Road.)

# WALK 8: EDERN — MADRYN CASTLE

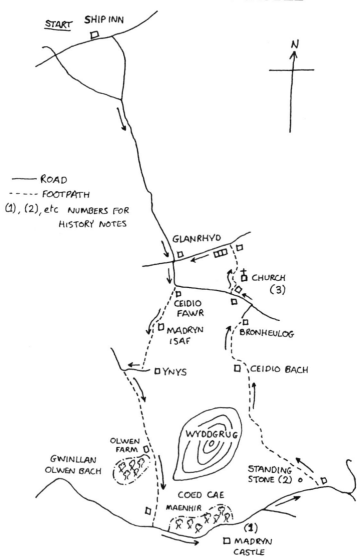

## Walk 8
# Edern — Madryn Castle

**3 hours**

*The following walk is a combination of footpaths and lanes and is quite straight forward, as it presents no difficult terrain.*

The best place to start is at the *Ship Inn* at the centre of Edern. Proceed down-hill from here taking the first right in about 100 metres. Carry on down the lane until after about 1 mile you will come to a crossroads, go straight on here until you reach a house called Ceidio Fawr where you will turn right through a large white field gate onto a footpath. Opposite the house cross over the wooden stile and carry straight on through a gap in the hedge in about 50 metres. Keep roughly to the left hand side of the field, cross over a broken footbridge and then turn right, continuing in the direction of the next farm called Madryn Isaf and staying near the field boundary.

The small hill on your left nearest to you is called Wyddgrug and on its summit was an Iron Age settlement. You will pass closer to this later on in the walk.

Cross over a wooden step stile and turn left.

If the field has its annual barley crop keep to the boundary on the left and follow it round, if not, cut straight across the field keeping just right of the house.

Cross at the stile in front of the house and proceed ahead at right angles to the stile past the house, now on your left, and into a small green lane. At the end of this lane you will come to a broken gate, climb over this and head down the field alongside the fence on your left.

About 150 metres before the corner of the field there is a stile, hidden almost completely by the undergrowth, cross this, taking care on the other side as there are some steps hidden by greenery (we missed them).

Turn right here onto the lane and after about 150 metres turn left on the sharp bend into a green lane and continue.

Cross the wooden step stile and head for Olwen farm in the distance, keeping to the edge of the field. At the field gate, cross the wooden step stile on the left and carry straight along the boundary following the stream.

The path is a very pleasant one, being liberally dotted with mature oak and beech trees. On your left is Coed Cae-Maen-Hir.

After a few hundred metres, cross over a stile and proceed into the farm yard of Olwen farm.

If the path to the left around the farm is blocked or very overgrown, as it was when we made the trip, go through the yard and over a stile. After crossing this stile turn left. At this point in front of you is Gwinllan Olwen Fach (*Little Olwen's Wood*).

Carry on around the field border until you find yourself opposite a house, turn into the field gate here and walk on to the next field gate, go through this and continue up the path, which after a short while emerges onto a road. Turn left here and continue. About halfway to the next turn off and unfortunately not visible from the road is a large house called Castell Madryn.[1]

After about ½ mile bear left off the main road onto a lesser road at the next junction and continue. Just before the house called Ger yr Efail turn left onto a green lane and in a few metres cross over the stile into the next field which contains a standing stone,[2] turn right and head for the next stile, cross over this and follow the boundary until you come to another stile.

After crossing this and a foot bridge, skirt the field in front of you heading towards the left boundary. After a short walk, cross the next stile on your left and head towards the farm in the distance. Make towards the right of the building and cross the wooden step stile, go over the tarmac path across from the old farm building and over the wooden stile and continue at right angles to it.

After passing the house there is a reminder of days gone by in the shape of an old pigsty with its own small pigman's cottage attached.

After this, follow the field boundary on your right until after a while you will come across a wooden step stile, look straight across

*Tranquil scene in the heart of Llŷn*

*Standing stone near Ger yr Efail*

the field to the next stile. After this turn right onto a green lane, go through the gate at the farm and through the yard, turn left onto the lane and continue.

At the end of this lane turn left onto the road, after a while passing the old chapel and grave yard (Peniel, 1887). After the chapel turn right into Ty'n y Capel and after about 15 metres turn left over a stone step stile, continue, following the field boundary on your right where you will see Ceidio church.

Head towards the corner of the field at the rear of some houses and through the kissing gate into a totally overgrown path, which as a matter of interest my co author and I spent some time clearing, hope you wont have to do the same. Emerging eventually onto a road, you will make a left turn here, after about 300 metres take the turning for Edern and return to the Ship Inn.

## History Notes

[1] Madryn Castle was the home of the gentry family of Madryn who came to power in the 16th century. The present house dates, almost entirely from the 19th century. All that remains of the original building is a section of rough rubble walling at the back of the house. There is some 18th century fabric in the east wing. There is a gate-house which dates from the early part of the 17th century.

[2] The standing stone in this field was probably erected in the late Neolithic or early Bronze Age, not a lot can be said with certainty standing stones in general (Llŷn has several). Essentially we have no idea what they were for. An obvious suggestion was that they were burial markers, Neolithic gravestones, and whereas, some on excavation have proved to be associated with burials this is not the case for the majority. So if they were not burial sites in the primary sense, what were they? Many people over the last couple of centuries have offered explanations, some more credible than others, but the idea which forms the basis of many modern theories and is highly controversial among archaelogists was begun back in the 1920's by Alfred Watkins. This man was a walker, rambler,

and writer, and it was during a walk while resting on a section of high ground, he had what amounted to a visionary experience. He pictured in his mind the land laid out before him with various and assorted features, including standing stones, all interconnected by straight lines. Thus was born, or rather re-born, the concept of 'ley lines' as Watkins called them. He subsequently published his exhaustive work on ley's in a now famous book called *The Old Straight Track*. The hunt for ley lines was on! It became quite a fashionable pursuit for walking and rambling societies, historians, archaelologists (usually trying to disprove them), antiquarians and the generally curious. Watkins did not know what these ley lines were, he came up with the logical-seeming theory that they were way-markers for prehistoric trackways. But as interest grew in these enigmatic alignments it became apparent that, if they were marking travel routes, some of these routes were very inconvenient indeed, passing, as they did, through the centres of lakes, over inaccessible peaks, swamps, and straight off the edges of cliffs!

We still do not know what ley lines are, but we can see them on maps. Anyone equipped with an O.S. map of virtually any area in Britain, and a ruler, can plot ley lines. If you mark on the map all the positions of standing stones you will notice that by application of a straight edge many of the stones fall into alignment. You will notice also that many old churches also occur on these lines. These lines, after diligent work, can be seen to criss-cross all over the place. True, many lines will occur on the map purely by chance, but usually far too many can be found to be accounted for by change alone. Other features which commonly turn up on ley lines include, stone circles, burial mounds, barrows, tumuli, dolmens, cromlechs etc., and any other similar, related or equivalent sites. Many natural features such as mountain tops, which were often crowned with a cairn, also occur on leys. The explanation for the occurrence of churches on ley lines is to be sought in the fact that most church sites (if not all) which are demonstrably ancient were placed on previous pagan sacred sites. The policy of the Christian Church when founding a new church in a certain pagan locality would be to choose the existing site of worship used by the people.

It was an attempt to demonstrate that the new religion had vanquished and replaced the old, and at the same time continuing to acknowledge the sanctity of the site itself.

Modern theories, in attempting to explain ley lines, whilst retaining the central feature of the alignments themselves, as demonstrated by Watkins, have reached conclusions differing widely in imagination, likelihood and general acceptability. Most of these theories revolve around the idea of the lines as being energy carriers of some sort, natural earth-energy that manifests itself in straight lines, or a grid like pattern, on the Earths' surface (it should be noted that ley lines occur all over the Earth, not just Britain). Theory has it that our ancestors had some technique, now lost to us, of concentrating this earth energy at certain points, and these points were marked by standing stones etc. The accumulated ley energy could be tapped at these points by tribal 'wizards' or 'shamans' and used for the benefit of the tribe as a whole. For example: helping in the growth of crops or healing the sick. This latter function, indeed, has echoes in folk-lore were there are legends attached to many stones attributing to them the ability to cure the sick. Other attributes are often attached to these stones in folk-lore, such as the ability to move, speak, drink at a nearby river, predict the identity of a future marriage partner and many other wonderful things such as concealing buried treasure. These beliefs are the remnants in folk-beliefs of the times when these stones and similar sites were known to harbour energy, a real 'treasure' if used wisely. Most modern-day dowsers insist that the ley system is still active today, with energy present at nearly all ley sites, but that the system is in a very broken-down state and is a feeble echo of what it must once have been. The stone here is on a ley line which includes another stone about a quarter of a mile distant at Meillionen farm (see note 4, Walk 10, 'Edern — Madryn Castle'). (For more on ley lines see history note 4, Walk No 8, 'Mynydd Mawr — St Mary's Chapel' in the companion volume to this.)

[3] Ceidio Church stands within a raised circular churchyard and is mentioned in 1254 in a document known as the 'Valuation of

Norwich'. It is individual in construction and is 10 metres long and 5 metres wide. The west gable with the doorway and bell-cote are modern and the upper courses of stone work in the walls have been rebuilt. The roof contains arch braced trusses dating from around 1500. There is an old grave in the churchyard to Grace Meredeth 1699.

Inside the church is a brass tablet with the inscription 'Sarah E.M. Williams-Jones-Parry, of Madryn Castle, restored this church in memory of her beloved brother, Sir T. Love D. Jones-Parry 15th Sept 1897'. There is a long, round stone baptismal font set in the wall of the church 'probably one of the oldest in existence in Wales — dating back to early days of Christianity when baptism by immersion was general'.

The church yard is the burial place of the bard Twm Pedrog renowned for his fine *englynion* as well as being remembered for taking part in a whale fishing trip, in which amidst bad weather conditions, a very close approach to the North Pole was made.

The Church is described thus by Edmund Hyde-Hall:

'The Church is a small building, and is remarkable only, as far as I could learn, for being without a register — an omission at once so mischievous and so easily supplied that it can scarcely be too much reprobated. Within is set up a tablet to the memory of Owen Jones, described as an eminent proficient in arithmetic, who perished in a voyage from Halifax to Liverpool in 1804. The burst of ambitious acquirement is always grateful to me, and the notice of this young man's progress in so useful and acceptable a branch of knowledge must be useful if it excites emulation' (but not if you emulate his nautical exploits!).

# WALK 9: EDERN — GARN FADRYN

— ROAD
- - - - FOOTPATH
(1), (2), etc. NUMBERS FOR HISTORY NOTES

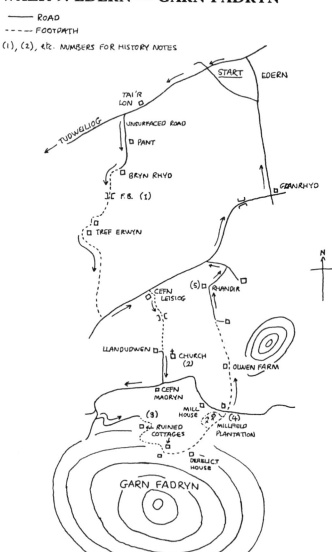

# Edern — Garn Fadryn

**4 hours**

*This walk for the most part is over fairly easy terrain with a hilly section at mid-point.*

*For parking, the best place is at the top of the village about 1/3 of a mile past the pub on the way out to Tudweiliog. Just before you leave the village there is a layby on the left.*

Start to walk out of the village on the main road and at the second left, at a farm called Bryn Rhyd, turn into the lane and follow this until the farm itself. At the farm yard turn right and then left and head across the big field in front of you, heading for the telegraph pole 200 metres down the field just to the right of Garn Fadryn.

On reaching the pole make your way to the edge of the field keeping slightly to the right of bushes and you will come across a foot bridge.[1] After crossing this, make your way towards the farm in front of you called Tref-erwyn. After crossing a couple of small streams head in the direction of the old tin barn to the right of the farm and enter the field gate in front of it, if it is locked, climb over and turn immediately left and make towards the farmhouse, leaving by a gate from which you will emerge onto a lane, turn left here and continue along the lane for about ¾ mile until you meet the road, where you will make a left turn.

After a few metres turn into the gateway on your right leading to Cefn Leisiog farm, and keeping left of the farmhouse, go through the yard leaving by a field gate on the right which leads into a field. Turn right in front of the 'bunker' and head towards the far corner of the field, about 200 metres. Here you will cross a stile and a small foot bridge. Keep to the right of the field following the boundary to the next gate. Go through the field gate and head off down a green lane coming in a short time to Llandudwen farm, here you proceed along the lane straight past the farm. Immediately after the farm you will see a small church on your left called 'St Tudwen's'.[2] This

*The path you have walked*      *The path you have yet to walk*

is well worth a small detour, it is possible that the keys to this church are held at the farm but we cannot confirm this. At the gate is a mounting block with the letters Carreg Farch inscribed upon it.

After visiting the church, continue down the lane, where in front and above you the imposing bulk of Garn Fadryn overlooks your progress.

On emerging onto the road turn right and continue for a while on this road, after the turning for Tudweiliog on your right, take the next left into a small tarmaced lane, after a short walk you will come to some houses, probably unchanged since the last century, where the tarmac road ends. Continue past these and start your climb up the hill on a small unsurfaced lane practically littered with deserted cottages all the way to the top.[3] Keep heading in an upward direction until you come to the end of the lane at a cottage called Pen-y-Gongl, go through the field gate and turn left continuing on this path for about 200 metres, on your right are two more examples of cottages declining into dereliction. After passing these houses and going through what used to be a field gate, the path splits, we will take the lower one heading downhill.

At the next fork above the woods[4], take the one to the right, climb over the wall and continue along the path passing above the woods and eventually heading down to the corner of the field, crossing a stile and emerging onto the road, Immediately across the road you will see a drive leading down to a cottage, before you reach the cottage you will see a field gate in front of you. Go through this and head towards another field gate by a house, pass over to the right hand field boundary, follow this down towards some woods and just before these you will see a stile. Cross this and bear left into the farm yard of Olwen farm, across the yard and in a short distance, you will see the next stile. The tree-lined path then proceeds for a ¼ of a mile or so. At the next stile leading into a field, turn right towards the gate in the corner and cross the stile next to it, head up the green lane for about 50 metres until it joins a tarmaced lane.

Turn left onto this lane and continue on, passing a farm called 'Rhandir'[5], after a while the lane emerges onto another track, turn left here and proceed down the lane for a few hundred metres turning right when you reach the main road. After ½ mile turn left at the crossroads into the turning for Edern. After about ½ a mile, just before Edern, turn left into Lôn Rhos, (if you pass a house called Caer Odyn you have gone too far). After a further 300 metres turn left onto a footpath which will bring you out onto the main road just below where your car is parked.

## History Notes

[1] From here as we proceed southward we enter the small inland parish of Llandudwen which is briefly described in *A Description of Caernarfonshire (1809-1811)*:

'This small parish is bounded on the north by Capel Ceidio, on the east by Bodean, on the south by Llaniestyn, and on the west by Tydweiliog. Of a clayey soil, it exhibits some flat and more sloping surfaces, well adapted to the purposes of decorative plantation. Of this disposition advantage has been judiciously taken around

*Llandudwen church*

*Llandudwen church from the east*

Madryn, the seat of Jones [sic] Parry Jones Esqr., where the wood is both florid and extensive.'

[2] This church is of extremely ancient foundation possibly mid 5th century. The original foundation was over the grave of St Tudwen who had fled from persecution. St Tudwen was the daughter of a Dark Age ruler named Brychan. Her sister Meleri was grandmother of the Patron Saint of Wales, St David.

Unusually for this area the churchyard is rectangular. The building itself is also of unusual plan which is the result of successive rebuildings, the earliest being in 1595. From this period also, dated the nave, but an earlier part of the church may have been incorporated in the west end. Also of the 16th century is the north transept, whilst the south transept dates to the early 17th century.

The church is approached through a large and impressive lychgate which was restored in 1907 and again in 1958. Near the outer gate is a large and fine example of a mounting block bearing the inscription Carreg Farch, a nice reminder of the days of more environmentally friendly transport! The lychgate along with the mounting block probably belongs to the 18th century.

The octagonal gritstone font is certainly mediaeval and may be as early as the 10th century.

Within the north transept is a memorial slab to Gaynor Griffith of Nyffryn (a nearby farmhouse) 1670. In the south transept is a memorial to Owen Williams 1733. The church also possesses a fine silver chalice made around 1500.

Llandudwen church is now a tidy, well maintained building. This was emphatically not the situation a couple of centuries ago:

'Divine service is celebrated, only once a fortnight by the rector of Rhiw, who comes over from his own parish on the stated days. The condition of the building itself is deplorable. The west end of the roof has fallen in, the south window was totally denuded of glass and that in the north wall was so entirely encrusted over by a colony of snails that the light was altogether excluded. It was also easy to observe that the pulpit, desk, etc., were roosting places for all sorts of fowl.'

[3] This path which is still listed on the O.S. map as being suitable for vehicles may perhaps call to mind the kind of roads encountered by Edmund Hyde-Hall in his travels when he states in his section on Llandudwen parish the following:

'The roads which pass through the parish are at present such as may suffice for communications of necessity. They are not very judiciously led, and their construction is not sufficiently firm to resist the effects of heavy rains upon the clayey soil. In truth there is not yet in this part of the country commerce enough to encourage and maintain roads of easy passage.'

There will be noticed a ruined cottage to the side of the track and another at the top of the track on the left. These couple of cottages along with the more substantial farm house called Tŷ Uchaf (*upper house*) a few hundred metres from the end of the track are sad and evocative reminders of a small crofting/farming community that for some reason was abandoned. If we regard the still-lived-in cottages at the bottom of the track where the macadamed road ended as part of the same community, strung out along the road on

*Derelict farm house high on the flanks of Garn Fadryn*

its winding ascent of the flanks of Garn Fadryn, we have the odd situation of a small village or hamlet, the 'top half' of which has died and the lower part has survived.

[4] The wood below the path at this point is called 'millfield plantation'. The large building at the bottom of the valley was in the last century, a flourishing mill, called Melin Madryn.

[5] The name Rhandir (as explained earlier) is a reference to the ancient Welsh customs of land inheritance.

# WALK 10: BODUAN — HALL AND PARISH

———— ROAD

- - - - - FOOTPATH

(1),(2), etc. NUMBERS FOR HISTORY NOTES

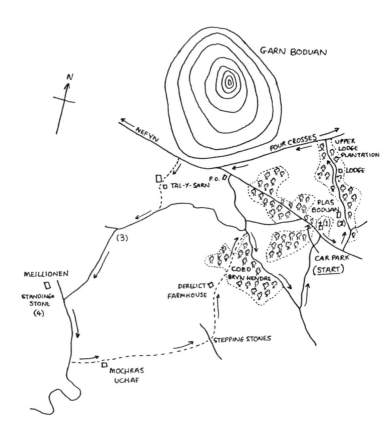

GARN BODUAN

N

NEFYN

FOUR CROSSES

UPPER LODGE PLANTATION

LODGE

P.O.

TAL-Y-SARN

PLAS BODUAN

(1) (2)

(3)

CAR PARK (START)

MEILLIONEN

STANDING STONE (4)

COED BRYN HENDRE

DERELICT FARMHOUSE

STEPPING STONES

MOCHRAS UCHAF

# Walk 10
# Boduan Hall and Parish

**4 hours**

*For ease of parking you should head for the layby at AA box No 580 near to Boduan church,[1] on the main Pwllheli-Nefyn road. (Map reference SH 3242 3780). The following walk is different in many respects to the previous walks as it will take you through one of the most heavily wooded areas of the Llŷn. This is a fairly easy walk and apart from one area that is usually wet there are no particular problems in completing it.*

Leave the car park and turn left onto the main road, take the next left and after about 150 metres take the left fork and follow this delightfully wooded lane[2] for about ¾ mile until it meets up with the main road. Turn left here and in 1/3 mile the road rejoins the main Nefyn — Pwllheli road, turn right and in a couple of hundred metres turn left at the footpath sign for Rhydyclafdy and Llanbedrog, which is opposite a few houses. Enter the small wrought iron gate and proceed down a flight of steps and in about 25 metres climb a wooden step stile, head down the slope in the direction of a wooden foot-bridge. After crossing this, make towards the farm (Tal-y-Sarn) on a hill in front of you.

Cross over a wooden step stile and head past the small farm house on your left following the path through a field gate and continue down this track. At the end of the track where it meets a tarmac road turn right. Proceed along this lane until arriving at a junction where you will bear left.[3] After about 1/3 of a mile you will arrive at another road junction where you will turn left. (At this point you may if you wish make a slight detour to see the standing stone, if so, turn right and in about 50 metres you will see it in a field on your left. Retrace your steps and continue down the small road.)[4]

Head along this road until a sign for Mochras Isa, turn into this lane and continue through the field gate following the path. This path is fairly wet and it may be necessary to detour into a field to get around the larger pools, there are gates into and out of the field enabling you to do this.

After a while you will come to two field gates side by side take the right one and continue until you meet up with a small brook, you will have to ford this on small stepping stones and climb up the opposite bank stepping over a small fence.

Turn left, and following the field boundary on your left, head in the direction of the old ruined house, there is a small stream running beside the house from the woods above and behind, the best place to cross this will be found 30 or 40 metres up the slope immediately before the woods, this may be a little boggy but quite crossable.

*Ruined farm house*

Make towards the top of the field. Go 'under!' the field gate unless they have repaired or replaced it. Continue along the path which leads through the woods.

At the end of the path it will emerge onto a tarmac road where you will turn right.

After 1/3 of a mile and in a field on your left is what looks like a small standing stone, but is probably a livestock rubbing post.

Turn off at the next left at the staggered junction opposite 'Mathan Isaf' where at the end of this road you will re-emerge on the main road virtually at your starting point.

## History Notes

[1] This church was newly constructed in the time of Edmund Hyde-Hall's visit to the parish in the first decade of the 19th century, he describes it thus:

'The building is cruciform and of recent erection through the bounty, as I understand, of the first Lord Newborough's aunts. The construction, however, by no means recalls the solidity of ancient masonry, for it is already in decay, and the vault itself, which ought to be the durable mansion of many generations, exhibits such signs of ruin that no man can venture upon it without incurring the danger of an untimely entombment. With respect to the monuments, if there be not much statuary, there is at least a respectable display of sculpture illustrated by the blazonry of various achievements. The loss of my notes clouds too much any account I could have given of this districts particulars, but I know not that I lament the accident on any account more than the disability it occasions of describing the family histories from these marble documents.'

So, we are not the only authors to lose notes! The church, undoubtedly due to its crumbling state, was totally rebuilt in 1894 by the architect Henry Kennedy. Some of the fixtures and fittings from the earlier church were kept and incorporated into the new building, such as (1) two bells dated 1754 and 1774. (2) Parish register (commencing 1679). (3) Silver chalice bearing the inscription 'The Parish of Bodvean. Drinke yee all of itt. Math:26:ver:27.' and with a London date-letter for 1623-4. (4) Silver paten-cover dated 1623. (5) Large goblet-shaped silver chalice bearing the inscription 'The gift of St John Wynn Bart. to

149

the church of Bodvean Anno 1772.' (6) A silver alms dish engraved with the inscription 'The Gift of Sr John Wynn Bart/1769.

We can aid Edmund Hyde-Hall and supply some of the information contained in these 'marble documents'. There is a memorial in the form of a marble tablet in the north transept to Griffith Wynn of Boduan (1680). In the west porch is a marble urn on a pedestal to Sir William Wynn, second son of Griffith Wynn with the inscription 'was interred 24th May, 1754. At Bodvean' (added later). There is a marble table-tomb in the north transept dedicated to the same person and also a table-tomb and casket to Sir John Wynn (2nd) Bt., 1773. In the church yard there is a gravestone to John Wynn 1635, grandson of John Wyn of Bodfel; also to his son Thomas Wynne 1673.

2 The woods which surround Boduan Hall today are a small remnant of a large forest which was a hunting ground for Tudor nobility. Perhaps, in modern times, this remnant has not diminished a great deal more than in the time of Hyde-Hall when he was able to say:

'The appearance of the parish is in general cheerful — more cheerful by contrast, from the hedgerows and woods pretty generally discernable. But the chief object in this respect is the florid plantation about Boduan Hall, and the more aged avenue from the house to the church.'

He then goes on to describe the hall:

'The Hall of Plas Boduan, though now a building of small pretension, has long been the seat of the ancient family of the Wynnes. Of this family, exceeded in point of antiquity, I presume by few within the kingdom, this place was long the customary abode; but when it became possessed by marriage of the great Glynne property . . . , a more commodious residence and a more accessible situation so far prevailed, it is probably, to induce the desertion of the ancient mansion in favour of the recent acquisition. Lord Newborough, the present representative of the united families, has been for several years, and still is, a minor, a circumstance that cannot fail to make a fortune already great among the very first within the county.'

The house to which Hyde-Hall was referring in the last quotation was built in 1736. The present much larger house incorporating the earlier one is of two and three storeys, and dates mostly from the late 19th century.

[3] A brief note here of some modern history. Until two or three years ago the grassy bank 70 metres or so from the road behind the gates was the county rubbish tip, a huge sprawling area, unsightly and stinking. A commendable job has been done in removing all visible traces of the tip by the local council. A nice instance of the all-too-rare situation of landscape enhancement in these modern times of 'progress'.

[4] Here is another fine example of a standing stone. For a discussion of the subject of standing stones in general, see history note 8 on Walk 8 'Edern — Madryn Castle'. (And in the companion volume to this in note 4, Walk 8, Mynydd Mawr — St Mary's chapel.)

*Standing stone at Meillionen*

# Books For Further Reading

For those readers whose interest may have been stimulated by some of the wide ranging historical and archaelogical subjects raised and briefly touched upon in these two books, or for those who wish to pursue some of these subjects in greater detail, here is a list of books which will prove helpful.

### 1. General works covering a wide range of periods and subjects

*The Royal Commission of Ancient and Historical Monuments in Wales:* Caernarfonshire vols I, II and III. Out of print but absolutely invaluable, can be consulted through the library service.

*Atlas of Caernarvonshire (Gwynedd Rural Council):* Brief but excellent on wide range of subjects from the prehistoric to the modern.

*History of Caernarfonshire (A.H. Dodd):* Highly readable general account of county history, beginning with Edwardian Conquest up to modern times excellent for 18th and 19th centuries.

*History of Gwynedd (Dorothy Sylvester):* Covers all subjects, good maps, drawings and photographs.

*Gwynedd Anthology (Ian Skidmore):* Miscellany of notes impressions and reflections on all subjects in all ages. Extremely entertaining.

*Across the Bardsey Sound:* A short informative book on the history of Bardsey.

*Enlli (Peter Hope Jones, editor):* A fascinating photographic record of life on Bardsey.

*Edern a Porthdinllaen (Iona Roberts):* Absorbing series of three photographic books on the village life, and characters of Edern.

*Pwllheli (D.G. Lloyd Hughes):* Excellently researched and well written account of the history of the town.

### 2. Prehistoric and Archaelogical

The Royal Commission books (see above)

*Wales: An Archaelogical Guide (Christopher Houlder):* Good basic guide to all periods.

*Celtic Britain (Lloyd Laing):* Excellent photographs and a well written account of the archaelogical aspect of the Celts in Britain.

*Origins of Britain (Lloyd and Jenefer Laing):* Similar treatment to the above book but devoted to the Palaeolithic, Neolithic and Bronze Age.

### 3. Celtic and Dark Ages

*And Shall These Mute Stones Speak? (Charles Thomas):* An excellent book covering the subject of Christian inscribed stones of the Dark Ages in western Britain.

*The Age of Arthur: A History of the British Isles from 350-650 (John Morris):* A 'magnum opus' account of the period, a large book with all the details.

*Wales in the Early Middle Ages (Wendy Davies):* One of the best books for Dark Age Wales.

*The Celts (Norah Chadwick):* Excellent book on the historical aspect of the Celts as opposed to the purely archaelogical.

*Wales before 1066 — A Guide (Donald Gregory):* Covering the period from the prehistoric to the Norman Conquest, good for the Dark Age period, a good introductory account.

### 4. Mediaeval

*Journey Through Wales and Itinery of Wales (Gerald of Wales):* A translation by Lewis Thorpe, of the original works of Gerald, highly readable.

*Giraldus Cambrensis (Michael Richter):* A published Phd thesis on Gerald of Wales. All the detail of his life and works.

*A Mirror of Mediaeval Wales (Charles Kightly):* A commemorative book for the 800th anniversary of Gerald of Wales' tour round Wales. An excellent book with full colour photographs, drawings and paintings.

*The Thirteenth Century (Sir Maurice Powicke):* A volume in the definitive Oxford History of England series but treats fully of the 'Welsh Scene' in this century.
*The Governance of Gwynedd (D. Stephenson):* Covers the administrative and political situation in Gwynedd in the time of the Welsh princes.

*The Age of Conquest: Wales 1066-1415 (R.R. Davies):* Simply the best.

### 5. King Arthur

*Journey to Avalon (Chris Barber and David Pykitt):* Indispensable for the new research on Arthur, especially for the Llŷn peninsula.

*The Arthur of the Welsh: (Edited by Rachael Bromwich, A.O.H. Jarman and Brinley F. Roberts):* A thorough research by various authors into the references to Arthur occurring in mediaeval Welsh literature.

*The Quest for Arthurs Britain (Geoffrey Ashe, editor):* Excellent guide to the 'Arthur Sites' in England and Wales.

### 6. Church and Religion

*The Welsh Church From Conquest to Reformation (Glanmore Williams):* A tour deforce by one of Wales' foremost historians.

*Saints Seaways and Settlements (E.G. Bowen):* Excellent treatment of the seaways and routes used by 6th and 7th saints in the Irish sea, also the nature of their settlements.

*Literature Religion and Society in Wales 1660-1730 (Geraint H. Jenkins):* Exhaustively researched and highly readable account of the subject of religious literature during the Restoration period, covers established church literature and nonconformist literature, it is an excellent book for charting the development of nonconformism in Wales.

*Lives of the Welsh Saints (Canon Doble):* Highly acclaimed hagiography of the 5th and 6th century saints.

*Lives of the British Saints (Baring Gould and John Fisher, edited by Derek Bryce):* Interestingly written lives of numerous British saints of the early Dark Age period.

## 7. The 'Modern' Period

*History of Caernarfonshire (A.H. Dodd):* (See above)

*The Industrial Revolution in North Wales (A.H. Dodd):* The definitive book on this subject.

*Atlas of Caernarfonshire:* (See above)

*History of Gwynedd (Dorothy Silvester):* (See above)

*Modern Wales a Concise History c.1485-1979 (Gareth Elwyn Jones):* Covers political, social and economic issues.

*Pwllheli (D.G. Lloyd Hughes):* Scholarly work on the general history of the town, mainly the 19th century.

## 8. Maritime

*Porthmadog Ships (Aled Eames and Emrys Hughes):* A superb study of the ships of Porthmadog and Llŷn.

*Immortal Sails (Henry Hughes):* Another fine study of the maritime history of Porthmadog.

*Growing Up Among Sailors (J. Ifor Davies):* An evocation of the maritime history of Nefyn.

*Pwllheli — The Port and Mart of Llŷn (Lewis Lloyd):* A history of the town concentrating on the 19th century maritime story.

*Anglesey and Llŷn Shipwrecks (Ian Skidmore):* Photographs, drawings and description of some of the better known shipwrecks.

*History of the Porthdinllaen Lifeboats:* The full story, well written.

## 9. Architecture etc.

*Vernacular Architecture (R.W. Brunskill):* Building styles, techniques and dating methods of all 'peasant' architecture.

*Welsh Historic Monuments (CADW):* A series of individual guides to abbeys, castles etc. and other monuments in public care, published by the Ministry of Works.

*Houses of the Welsh Countryside (P. Smith):* A monumental study of all house types of all ages, under the aegis of the Royal Commission of Ancient and Historical Monuments. Superb and numerous line-drawings in graphic detail along with a multitude of distribution maps. This is a huge book, not only in size.

*Mediaeval Stone Carving in North Wales. Supulchral Slabs and Effigies of the Thirteenth and Fourteenth Centuries. (C.A. Gresham):* The definitive work on this subject.

## 10. Folk Lore, Myths and Legends, Ley Lines, Standing Stones etc.

*Celtic Folklore (2 vols) (John Rhys):* Contains vast amount of personally collected folklore, mainly Welsh, and hugely interesting. Lots pertaining to Llŷn.

*Mysterious Wales (Chris Barber):* Myths, legends, strange stories and oddities from around Wales, lots of photographs.

*More Mysterious Wales (Chris Barber):* More of the same.

*Ancient Stones of Wales (Chris Barber):* Folklore legends and local myths associated with standing stones, cromlechs, stone circles etc., many photographs. Delves into ley lines.

*Needles of Stone (Paul Graves):* Ley lines and geomancy connected with standing stones.

*Quicksilver Heritage (Paul Screeton):* Still the best introduction to what ley lines are all about.

*Welsh Folk Lore (Owen):* Traditional folk customs from around Wales, presented in a scholarly fashion.

*The Mabinogion:* Available in several translations but that by Gwyn Jones and Thomas Jones has a nice archaic but readable quality.

## 11. Travel Writers of the Past

*A Description of Caernarfonshire (Edmund Hyde-Hall):* Available in a modern edition. You may feel as though you have read enough Hyde-Hall but it really is worth while reading the complete book. As a contemporary comment on the social, economical, agricultural and many other aspects of the condition of the county at the beginning of the 19th century this book is totally unique and priceless.

*Tours in Wales (Thomas Pennant):* As Hyde-Hall is unparalleled for the county of Caernarfonshire, Pennant is so for the whole of Wales in the late 18th century.

*Wild Wales (George Borrow):* This book, of a similar nature and stature to Pennant, covers Wales in the later 19th century and is superbly written.

## 12. Periodicals

*The Transactions of the Caernarfonshire Historical Society 1939:* Annually produced volume containing articles of a high standard on all conceivable subject relating to the history of the county in all periods. Can be purchased or consulted via the library service.

*Cymru a'r Môr/Maritime Wales 1976:* Another annually produced magazine featuring all aspects of Wales maritime history.

## Other walking books from Gwasg Carreg Gwalch

**The Mountain Walker's Guide to Wales** *192pp. £6.90 0-86381-154-X. Map; plastic protective cover.*

- describes 100 routes of varying lengths and difficulty from gentle strolls to tough excursions which covers 200 Welsh peaks
- contains something suitable for every category of walker
- includes virtually every mountain summit in Wales, many of which are represented in a guide for the first time
- covers every mountain group in Wales
- gives practical advice about safety and equipment
- provides fascinating geological, historical and general interest facts

*Colin Adams*

*Also available by the same authors:*

**Walks in the Snowdonia Mountains** *96pp. £1.80. 0-86381-065-9. Including accurate maps and drawings.*
This book describes 45 walks, mostly circular, varying in length from 3.5 km (2¼ miles) to 16 km (10 miles).
*Don Hinson*

**Walks in North Snowdonia** *96pp. £1.99. 0-86381-122-1. Including accurate maps and drawings.*
Over 400 km (250 miles) of routes are mapped and described, making the book exceptionally good value for money. There are also comments on a further 100 km of paths which should help those wishint to explore the area further.
*Don Hinson*

**New Walks in Snowdonia** *96pp. £2.75. 0-86381-265-1. Maps with every walk; pen & ink drawings.*
34 circular walks, together with many variations. This book introduces you to lesser known paths and places which guide book writers seem to have neglected. Surprisingly, some of these paths are in familiar areas such as the Snowdon range. There are walks for all kinds of walkers, specially chosen to reveal the natural beauty of the landscape.
*Don Hinson*

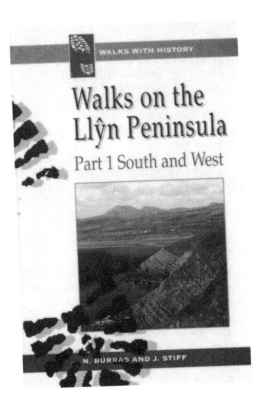

WALKS WITH HISTORY

# Walks on the Llŷn Peninsula

Part 1 South and West

N. BURRAS AND J. STIFF

# Walks in the Llŷn Peninsula

**Part 1 — South and West**

*Gwasg Carreg Gwalch — £4.50*